INTRODUCTION

Pronunciation

1 Accented syllables are stressed: al 'fândega.
2 In Portugal, stressed and unstressed syllables contrast very distinctly while in Brazil, each syllable is pronounced clearly and slowly in an even intonation.

Vowels:

a As in *cat*: mar, sapo

â, a When placed before nasal consonant; like *anglo*: cama, câmbio

á,à As in *cat* above: há, lá

e,é *Stressed:* like *sell*: ela, certo, pé, café

e *Unstressed* at beginning of word, like *i* in *linen*: escuro. esta

e *Unstressed* at the end of a word, often disappears: azeite, xaile

ê As *e* in *envy*: vê

i Like *y* in *yet*: fica, ali

o *Stressed:* Like *au* in *naughty*: boa, osso; or like *o* in *cod*: posso, agora.

o *Unstressed:* like *u* in *put*: carro, policia, comida

ó Like *a* in *small*: óculos, caracól

ô As in *naughty*: alô, vovô

u,ú Like *oo* in *moon*: uma, luta, música
Silent in **gu** and **qu** before **i** or **e**: quero, guerra

Nasal vowels Pronounced simultaneously through the nose and mouth.

ã, am, an Like *an* in *ranch*: irmã, banco.

ão Like *ow* in *crown* but nasalised: irmão, estão

ãe Like *ay* in *hay* but nasalised: mamãe.

Diphthongs The emphasis is on **a**, **e**, **o**, the strong vowels. **U** and **i** combine as a nasal diphthong: **ui** (m**ui**to).

ai Like *igh* in *high*: p**ai**, c**ai**'xa

au Like *ow* in *vow*: P**au**'lo, c**au**'le

ei Like *ay* in *may*: l**ei**'te

eu Like the *a* of *day* merging into the *oo* of *took* ('aoo'): m**eu**, t**eu**

ou Like *ow* in *bowl*: v**ou**

oi Like *oy* in *annoy*: l**oi**'ça, p**oi**s

Consonants Similar to English, but with the following exceptions:

c Before a consonant, or **a**, **o**, **u**, like *k* in *keep*: **c**orreio, **c**rédito. Before **e** and **i**, like *s* in *sand*: **c**éu, **c**inema

ç As *s* in *sand*: cal**ç**a, ma**ç**a

ch As *sh* in *shock*: **ch**amar, **ch**eio

g Before **e** or **i**, like *s* in *casual*: **g**elo. Otherwise, like *g* in *go*.

h Silent: **h**otel, **h**á

j Like *s* in *casual*: ho**j**e

lh As *ll* in *million*: ol**h**ar, mil**h**o

m At end of word, almost silent: be**m**, que**m**

nh Like *ni* in *onion*: vi**nh**o

qu Followed by **e** or **i**, like *k* in *Kent*: **qu**ero, **qu**em, **qu**inta. If followed by **a** like *c* in *cart*: a**qu**ário

r At begining of word: like Scottish *r*: **r**ua, **r**ei. In middle of word, like *r* in *cart*: ca**r**o, cu**r**to. At end of word: soft like *r* in *maker*: lava**r**, esta**r**, parti**r**

rr Like the strong, trilled Scottish *r*: soco**rr**o, ca**rr**o

s At beginning of word or after consonant, like the *s* in *see*: **s**enhor, pul**s**o. Between vowels, like *z* in *lazy*: va**s**o, ca**s**a. At end of word or syllable, as *sh* in *shy*: esta, vamo**s**

ss Like *s* in *see*

x At beginning of word, and sometimes between vowels, as *sh* in *shy*: **x**ícara, cai**x**a, bai**x**o. Like English *z* when **ex** comes before a vowel: **ex**igir

z When at end of word, sounds like *s* in *casual*: nari**z**

CONTENTS

Introduction
Pronunciation
1	Segunda-feira/Monday	Hello and goodbye	1
		Arriving at the hotel	7
		Ordering drinks and snacks	14
2	Terça-feira/Tuesday	Getting around	19
		Finding out the time	26
3	Quarta-feira/Wednesday	Public transport	30
		At the bank	33
		Buying postcards	36
4	Quinta-feira/Thursday	Going shopping	40
		Shopping for food	43
		A phone call	47
		Sightseeing	48
5	Sexta-feira/Friday	A visit to the doctor	52
		Camping plans	54
		Driving and breakdowns	58
6	Sábado/Saturday	At the seaside	61
		Describing the day	63
		Entertainment	66
		Eating out	68
7	Domingo/Sunday	Buying souvenirs	74
		Talking about things	75
		Thanks and packing	81

Key to exercises   84
English–Portuguese topic vocabularies   85
Portuguese–English vocabulary   91

ACKNOWLEDGEMENTS

The authors and publishers are grateful to J. Allan Cash Ltd for supplying photographs.

PORTUGUESE

Hilary Fleming
and
Iza Moneiro Rainbow

Series Editors

Sarah Boas and Shirley Baldwin

Headway · Hodder & Stoughton

INTRODUCTION

Portuguese in a Week is a short course in Portuguese which will equip you to deal with everyday situations when you visit Portugal or Brazil: shopping, eating out, asking for directions, changing money, using the phones and so on.

The course is divided into 7 units, each corresponding to a day in the life of the Evans family during their week in Portugal. Each unit begins with a dialogue, which introduces the essential language items in context. Key phrases are highlighted in the dialogues, and the phrasebook section which follows lists these and other useful phrases and tells you what they are in English.

Within the units there are also short information sections in English on the topics covered, sections giving basic grammatical explanations, and a number of follow-up activities designed to be useful as well as fun. Answers can be checked in a key at the back of the book.

ISBN 0 340 50002 6

First published 1989

Typeset by Gecko Limited, Bicester, Oxon.
Printed in Great Britain for Headway, a division of Hodder and Stoughton Publishers, Mill Road, Dunton Green, Sevenoaks, Kent by Richard Clay Ltd, Norwich

HELLO AND GOODBYE

▶ **Arrival**   When you arrive in Portugal you will find customs (Alfândega) and passport control no problem and easy to understand – as in any other member country of the EEC. Most information is given in English as well as in Portuguese. Most notices and signs will be in both languages.

muito prazer/pleased to meet you

Maria Evans (35) and her husband Frank (40), have come to Portugal to visit family and friends as they do most summers. They have two children, José (15) and Célia (8). Luis Pereira from a car-hire firm is there to meet them at Lisbon airport. They shake hands.

Luis:	**Olá, bom dia.** Meu nome é Luis Pereira, sou de "Intercar". **E o senhor Evans?**
Frank:	Sim. sou. **Muito prazer**, senhor Pereira. **Apresento-lhe** a minha mulher.
Maria:	Bom dia. Muito prazer em conhecê-lo, senhor.

Luis: Muito prazer, senhora. Aqui está o seu carro, senhores. É para uma semana, não é? Aqui tem as chaves.

Frank: Muito **obrigado.** O senhor é muito amável. Até a próxima segunda feira. **Adeus.**

Luis: Obrigado e adeus.

Saying hello

Olá, bom dia	Hello, good morning/good day
Boa tarde	Good afternoon (used after midday and until it begins to get dark)
Boa noite	Good evening, good night

Saying goodbye

Adeus	Goodbye (friendly way to say goodbye any time)
Até logo/até já	See you soon (perhaps the same day)
Até a próxima	Until next time
Até a próxima segunda feira	Until next Monday

Addressing people in Portuguese   You address a man as **senhor** (Mr) and a woman as **senhora** (Mrs), whether married or not. A young girl is **menina** and a boy is **menino**. It is normal to shake hands both when meeting someone for the first time and when greeting a friend or acquaintance you may have met earlier the same day. Note that there is a formal and an informal way of saying 'you'. In formal situations, use **o senhor** for a man and **a senhora** for a woman. When introducing a lady, one should say **a senhora dona** followed by her complete name. If introducing a man, say **o senhor**.

Meeting people

Meu nome é . . ./Sou . . .	My name is . . ./I am . . .
Qual é o seu nome? Como se chama?	What is your name?
É o senhor Evans?	Are you Mr Evans?
Sim, sou eu.	Yes. I am
Apresento-lhe . . .	May I introduce you to . . .
o meu marido, a minha mulher	my husband, my wife
o meu amigo, a minha amiga	my friend (male, female)
a senhora dona Maria Evans	Mrs Maria Evans
o senhor Frank Evans	Mr Frank Evans
Muito prazer	Pleased to meet you
Não é?	Isn't it, aren't you, etc.

Saying 'Yes please' and 'No thank you'

Se faz favor/faz favor/por favor	Please
(muito) obrigado	Thank you (very much) (man)
(muito) obrigada	Thank you (very much) (woman)
Sim, por favor	Yes, please
Sim, obrigado (obrigada)	Yes, please
Não, obrigado (obrigada)	No, thank you
De nada/Não tem de que	Don't mention it

Other useful phrases

O senhor é (muito) amável	You are (very) kind (to a man)
A senhora é (muito) amável	You are (very) kind (to a woman)
Aqui está/estão (plural)	Here is/are
Aqui tem	Here you have, here it is

the way it works

People and things

In Portuguese, words for both people and things are either masculine or feminine. The word for 'the' is **o** for a masculine word (**o senhor** = the man, **o carro** = the car), and **a** for a feminine word (**a senhora** = the lady, **a chave** = the key).

Most words ending in **-o** are masculine (**o** amig**o** = boy friend, **o** filh**o** = son), and most words ending in **-a** are feminine (**a** filh**a** = daughter, **a** amig**a** = girl friend). But there are several other endings, and it helps to learn each new word with its **o** or **a**. You won't always be right but you will usually be understood!

To make a word plural

o > os   a > as

1   Add **-s** if the word ends in a vowel: **o** carr**o** – **os** carr**os** (the car, the cars); **a** senhora – **as** senhor**as** (the lady, the ladies)

2   Add **-es** if the word ends in a consonant: **o** senh**or** – **os** senh**ores** (the man, the men)

These are general rules but there are exceptions which will have to be noted as you meet them.

To Be

In the dialogue you met two verbs meaning 'to be': **ser** and **estar**.

3

Ser (Who are you?/What are you?)

Sou Luis Pereira   I am Luis Pereira
*É muito amável   You are very kind
Frank é Inglês   Frank is English
Ela é Portuguesa   She is Portuguese

*note: **é** can be used to say 'you are', 'she is', 'he is', and 'it is'.

This is what the verb **ser** looks like in the present tense (note the different ways of saying 'you'):

singular

(eu)	sou	I am
(tu)	és	you are (intimate)
(êle/ela)	é	he/she/it is
(o senhor)	é	you are (polite, masculine)
(a senhora)	é	you are (polite, feminine)
(você)	é	you are (friendly, all)

plural

(nós)	somos	we are
(os senhores)	são	you are (masc)
(as senhoras)	são	you are (fem)
(vocês)	são	you are (all)
(êles/elas)	são	they are

Use this verb for saying *who* you are and *what* you are. You can use it for:

1. Stating your nationality: **eu sou Inglês** (I am English)
2. Describing your appearance: **eu sou alto** (I am tall)
3. Describing your character: **eu sou inteligent** (I am intelligent)
4. Stating a relationship: **eu sou a mulher** (I am the wife)
5. Stating your occupation: **eu sou professor** (I am a teacher)
6. Saying where you are from: **eu sou de Londres** (I am from London)

Estar (How are you?/Where are you?)

Como está?   How are you? (singular)
(eu) Estou bem   I am well
Como estão êles?   How are they?
(êles) Estão bem   They are well

This is the second verb meaning 'to be'. Use this second verb for:

1. Saying how you are: **Estou bem** (I am well)
2. Saying where you are: **Estou em Lisboa** (I am in Lisbon)
3. Asking how people are: **Como está?** (How are you?)
   Como estão êles? (How are they?)
4. Saying where things are: **Aqui está/Aqui estão** (Here it is/Here they are)

This is its present tense:

singular			plural		
(eu)	estou	I am	(nós)	estamos	we are
(tu)	estás	you are	(os senhores)	estão	you are (masc)
(êle/ela)	está	he/she it is	(as senhoras)	estão	you are (fem)
(o senhor)	está	you are (polite, masc)	(vocês)	estão	you are (friendly, all)
(a senhora)	está	you are (polite, fem)			
(você)	está	you are (friendly, all)	(êles/elas)	estão	they are

My/your/his

We have met two examples of these possessive adjectives so far: a **minha** mulher (**my** wife), o **seu** carro (**your** car). This is how they are used:

1   The possessive adjective will be singular or plural, masculine or feminine, depending on the noun it is describing:

Masculine nouns (car)
o **meu** carro (**my** car)
os **meus** carros (**my** cars)
o **seu** carro (**his/her** car)
os **seus** carros (**his/her** cars)
o **nosso** carro (**our** car)
os **nossos** carros (**our** cars)

Feminine nouns (daughter)
a **minha** filha (**my** daughter)
as **minhas** filhas (**my** daughters)
a **sua** filha (**his/her** daughter)
as **suas** filhas (**his/her** daughters)
a **nossa** filha (**our** daughter)
as **nossas** filhas (**our** daughters)

Note: The adjective agrees in number (sing/plural) and gender (masc/fem) with the word it accompanies and not with the possessor.

Asking questions

This is quite straightforward and works in three different ways. You can:
1   Start with a question word:

como?	(how?)
onde?	(where?)
quem?	(who?)
qual?	(which?)
quanto?	(how much?)
quantos/quantas?	(how many?)

Como está?   How are you?
Qual é o seu filho?   Which is your son?

3   Make a statement but raise the pitch of your voice at
the end, and also your eyebrows!
Ela é a sua filha?   She is your daughter?

3   Again make a statement but add **não é?** (Isn't it, etc) at the end:
É para uma semana, **não é?**   It's for a week. isn't it?
Êle é o seu filho, **não é?**   He is your son, isn't he?

Negative statements

If you want to make a negative statement, put **não** immediately before the verb:
Éle **não** é o meu filho   He is not my son

things to do

Maria and Frank are in Customs. How do they answer the customs officer?

Funcionário: Os seus passaportes, por favor. São os senhores Evans?

1.1 Frank: ....
Funcionário: São seus filhos?

Maria: ....
Funcionário: É a sua mala (suitcase), não é?

Maria e Frank: ....
Funcionário: A chave, se faz favor.

Frank: ....
Funcionário: Obrigado.
Frank: ....

1.2 Use **ser** or **estar** to complete these statements.

1 Eu . . . a senhora Martins.
2 Nós . . . professôrës.
3 Êle . . . Inglês.
4 Êles . . . turistas (tourists).
5 Eu . . . Portuguesa.
6 Nós . . . em Portugal.
7 A senhora . . . amável.
8 Êle . . . de (from) Londres.

1.3 Choose the correct possessive adjective from the list below, and fill in the gaps. Don't forget that the gender (feminine/masculine) and number (singular/plural) must agree with the word:
meu/meus, minha/minhas, nosso/nossos, nossa/nossas, seu/seus, sua/suas

1 É   o . . . (mine) carro.
2 É   o . . . (your) nome?
3 É   a . . . (our) casa (house).
4 São os . . . (our) filhos.
5 É   a . . . (mine) mala.
6 São as . . . (your) chaves.

ARRIVING AT THE HOTEL

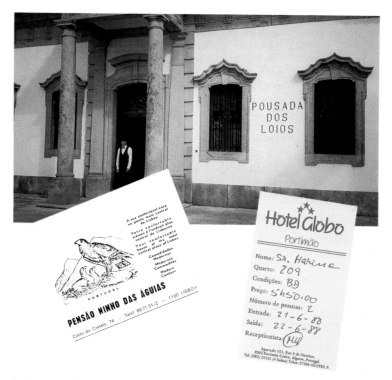

In Portugal, there are many kinds of accommodation. You can choose from a hotel, a **pensão** or **residencial** (bed and breakfast), or, if you are in one of the many historical towns, a **pousada** (a historical building converted into a hotel and run by the government). Guests are asked to fill in a registration form – **uma ficha**, on arrival, and may have to leave their passport at reception overnight.

aqui tem as chaves/here are the keys

That afternoon, Maria, Frank and the children arrive at their hotel in Lisbon and go to check in at the desk (**recepção**). Frank explains that they have already booked two rooms – one with twin beds and one double. He wants to know if there is a bathroom.

Frank: Boa tarde. Sou o senhor Evans. **Tenho dois quartos reservados**: um com duas camas e outro com cama de casal.

Recepcionista:	Ah. Sim! Sr. Evans, **faça o favor de** preencher esta ficha. (he fills in the form)
Recepcionista:	**Seu passaporte, se faz favor.** (he hands her his passport)
Recepcionista:	Obrigada. **Aqui tem** as chaves. São os quartos cinco (5) e sete (7) no segundo andar.
Maria:	Os quartos tem casa de banho?
Recepcionista:	Sim, tem.
Maria:	E **a que horas** servem o pequeno almoço?
Recepcionista:	O pequeno almoço é **das 8 horas às 10 horas.**
Maria:	Muito obrigada.
Recepcionista:	De nada. Até logo

Checking in

Tenho dois quartos reservados	I have reserved two rooms
um quarto com duas camas	one twin bedded room
. . . com cama de casal	a double room
Faça o favor de preencher esta ficha	Please fill in this form
Aqui tem as chaves	Here are the keys
no segundo andar	on the second floor
Tem?/Há?	Is there?/Are there?
Tem casa de banho?	Is there a bathroom?
Sim, há/Não, não há	Yes, there is/No, there isn't
A que horas servem. . .?	When (at what hour) do you/they serve. . .?
o pequeno almoço	breakfast
das oito(horas) às dez(horas)	from 8(o'clock) to 10(o'clock)

Booking accommodation

Há quartos vagos?	Are there any rooms free?
para duas noites	for two nights
. . . uma semana	. . . one week
. . . uma pessoa	. . . one person
com uma cama/duas camas/cama de casal	with single bed/twin beds/double bed
com casa de banho/chuveiro	with a bathroom/a shower
quarto e pequeno almoço	bed and breakfast
primeiro andar	first floor
posso ver o quarto?	can I see the room?

See the Topic Vocabulary on page 80 at the back of the book for numbers.

ORDERING DRINKS AND SNACKS

When in Portugal, you can have a drink at any time, in a bar (**o bar**) or a
cake and coffee shop (**a pastelaria**).

vamos tomar alguma coisa/let's have a drink

Before the evening meal, the Evans family go to the hotel bar.

Empregado:	Boa tarde, senhores. O que desejam tomar?
Frank:	Célia, o que queres tomar?
Celia:	Eu quero um sumo de laranja, pai.
Maria:	E tu, José, o que queres?
Jose:	Eu quero uma cola com gelo.

9

Frank:	Para mim, uma imperial, por favor. E tu, o que tomas, Maria?
Maria:	Um aperitivo de vinho do Porto, se faz favor.
Empregado:	Querem comer alguma coisa?
Frank:	Uhnn . . . uma dose de azeitonas verdes.
Maria:	E para mim, meia dose de queijo da Serra.

At the bar

O que desejam tomar (or **beber**)?	What do you want to drink? (polite, plural)
O que queres tomar?	What do you want to drink? (familiar, singular)

um sumo de laranja	an orange juice
pai/mãe	dad/mum
uma cola com gelo	a coca-cola with ice
e/é	and/is
para mim	for me
Querem comer alguma coisa?	Do you want to eat something?

As bebidas alcoólicas (Alcoholic drinks)

o vinho tinto/branco/rosé/verde	wine: red/white/rosé/'green' (from the Minho region)
o vinho do Porto	Port wine
o xerez sêco/doce/amontilhado	sherry: dry/sweet/medium
uma garrafa de vinho	a bottle of wine
meia garrafa de vinho	half bottle of wine
um copo de vinho	a glass of wine
uma cerveja	a beer
uma imperial	a draught lager
uma cerveja preta	a brown ale

As bebidas não alcohólicas (Non-alcoholic drinks)

àgua	water
um sumo de. . .	juice of. . .
laranja/limão/ananàs	orange/lemon/pineapple
um sumo natural	a freshly squeezed fruit juice
uma cola	a coca-cola
uma limonada	a lemonade
uma àgua mineral	a mineral water
um batido de chocolate/baunilha	a chocolate/vanilla milk-shake
um copo de leite	a glass of milk
um café com leite	a white coffee
um chá com leite	tea with milk
um chá com limão	tea with lemon
uma bica	a small black coffee

11

Os acepipes (Appetizers)

uma dose de . . .	a portion of . . .
meia dose de . . .	half portion of . . .
duas doses de . . .	two portions of . . .
azeitonas verdes/pretas	green/black olives
amêijoas	small clams
caracóis	snails
carnes frias	assorted cold meats
chouriço	smoked pork sausages (chorizo)
croquetes de bacalhau	cod croquettes
rissóis de camarão/galinha	deep fried pastry envelopes filled with prawns/chicken
linguiça frita	thin sliced fried chorizo
queijo da Serra	cheese from Serra da Estrela

Snacks

uma tosta mista	toasted cheese and ham sandwich
uma sandes de queijo	a cheese sandwich
uma sandes de fiambre/presunto	a cooked/smoked ham sandwich
um prego	a steak sandwich
um bolo	a slice of cake/a cake
um cachorro (dog)	a hotdog
uma hamburguesa	a hamburger

Ice creams

Um gelado de . . .	
morango	strawberry
baunilha	vanilla
chocolate	chocolate
nata	cream
laranja	orange
limão	lemon
ananás	pineapple

the way it works

Um, uma; dois, duas

The word for 'a' is **um** for masculine words, and **uma** for feminine words: **um** sumo (a juice), **uma** cerveja (a beer). Use **um/uma** also to say the number 'one'.

Likewise the number 'two' agrees with the gender of the word it accompanies: **dois quartos** (two rooms), **duas camas** (two beds).

Adjectives

Similarly, adjectives agree with what they are describing: **um** quart**o** pequen**o** (a small room), **uma** mal**a** pequen**a** (a small suitcase), **duas** cas**as** modern**as** (two modern houses), do**is** filh**os** pequen**os** (two small sons).

There is, there are

Note the following expressions from the second dialogue:

Há casa de banho?	Is there a bathroom?
Sim, há.	Yes, there is.

He could also have asked: **Há duas casas de banho?** (Are there two bathrooms?) This because **há** means both 'there is' and 'there are', *and* 'is there?', 'are there?'. Another way of saying **há** is **tem**: **Tem chuveiro?** (Is there a shower?).

Saying what you want

One of the first things you want to be able to say is 'I want'. You can do this by naming the object and adding **por favor** (uma cola, **por favor**) or you can use the verb **querer** (to want):

Quero uma cola	I want a coca-cola
Queremos uma garrafa de vinho	We want a bottle of wine

The present tense of the verb **querer** is as follows:

Singular			Plural		
(eu)	quero	I want	(nós)	queremos	we want
(tu)	queres	you want	(vocês)	querem	you want
(êle/ela)	quer	he/she wants	(os senhores)	querem	you want
(o senhor)	quer	you want	(as senhoras)	querem	you want
(a senhora)	quer	you want	(vocês)	querem	you want
(você)	quer	you want	(êles/elas)	querem	they want

things to do

1.4 Can you discover which answer goes with which question?

(a) O que quer o senhor?
(b) Como está, senhora dona Lurdes?
(c) Há casa de banho?
(d) Quem são êles?
(e) Carlos, quer comer alguma coisa?

1 São meus amigos
2 Quero um café, por favor.
3 Sim, há.
4 Não, obrigado.
5 Bem, obrigada.

GETTING AROUND

onde fica. . .?/where is. . .?

The Evans leave their hotel after breakfast and walk to Rossio railway station, where in the afternoon they will meet Maria's niece Cristina. They ask a passer-by for directions:

vire à direita/turn right

Frank:	Faz favor, **qual é o caminho** para a estação do Rossio?
Passante:	**Tome a primeira à esquerda** e **siga em frente** até a Av. da Liberdade. **Vire à direita** na Av. da Liberdade e a estação do Rossio está **à sua esquerda.**
Frank:	(smiling) **Mais devagar**, por favor.
Passante:	Tome a primeira à esquerda e siga em frente até a Av. da Liberdade. Vire à direita na Av. da Liberdade e a estação do Rossio fica à sua esquerda.
Frank:	Muito obrigado.
Passante:	De nada.

14

José is interested in monuments and historical buildings, and in Rossio they call at the Tourist Office (**O Turismo**).

José:	Bom dia. A senhora **tem** um mapa de Lisboa?
Funcionária:	Sim, **tenho. Aqui está.**
José:	Obrigado. **Onde fica** o Castelo de São Jorge?
Funcionária:	O Castelo de Sao Jorge **fica aqui à direita** (showing it on the map).
José:	Ah, sim! E a Av. da Liberdade, **é longe?**
Funcionária:	Não! **É muito perto! É aqui em frente**. O menino **só tem que atravessar** a Praça dos Restauradores
José:	Muito obrigado, minha senhora.
Funcionária:	De nada. Adeus.

Where is it?

Qual é o caminho para. . .?	Which is the way to. . .?
para a estação do Rossio	to the Rossio station
para a Catedral	to the Cathedral
para o Estoril	to Estoril
para o sul	to the south
vá/vai	go
dobre/vire/corte	turn
tome	take
siga/segue	follow
siga em frente	go straight on
até	till
primeira/última/próxima	first/last/next (fem)
primeiro/último/próximo	first/last/next (masc)
Onde fica. . .?/Onde é. . .?	Where is. . .?
o Turismo	the Tourist Office
o Castelo de São Jorge	St. George's Castle
a Praça dos Restauradores	the Restauradores Square
É/Fica. . .	It is. . .
aqui/ali/lá	here/there/there (further)
à direita/à esquerda	on the right/on the left
em frente (do, da)	in front (of the), facing
atrás (do, da)	behind (the)
ao lado (do, da)	beside (the)
longe (de, do, da)	far (from)
perto (de, do, da)	near (the)
muito longe/muito perto	very far/very near

15

Other useful phrases

só tem que . . .	you only have to . . .
atravessar . . .	to cross . . .
a rua	the street
a praça	the square
a avenida	the avenue
junto à	next to
à esquina	at the corner
na próxima esquina	at the next corner
até o fim	to the end
nos semáforos	at the traffic lights
do outro lado	on the other side
Tem um mapa . . .	Do you have a map. . .?
de Portugal	of Portugal
de Lisboa	of Lisbon
da cidade	of the city
do centro	of the centre

the way it works

Help! Help!

Desculpe, não percebo	Sorry, I don't understand
Pode/podia repetir?	Can/could you repeat that?
Mais devagar, por favor	More slowly, please
Mostre no mapa, se faz favor	Show me it on the map, please

Excuse me!

In the first dialogue, look at the way Frank calls the attention of the passer-by in order to ask him a question: **Faz favor**, qual é o caminho para o Rossio? You have already learned that the expression **faz favor** is one of the ways to say 'please'. Now you know that **faz favor** also means 'excuse me', when you want to attract someone's attention.

But, if in order to call the person's attention you have to *interrupt* a conversation or whatever the person is doing, you should say **desculpe** (I am sorry), so you will be at the same time, politely *apologising* for the interruption.

Where is it?

To find out where places are, start the phrase with the question **onde é** or **onde fica** followed by the subject in question:

Onde é a sua casa?   Onde é a estação?
Onde fica o Castelo?   Onde fica a rua Silveira Pessôa?

Ficar

You are familiar with two verbs in Portuguese meaning 'to be' – **ser** and **estar**. **Ficar** is the third verb 'to be' and it is interchangeable with **ser** only when used to explain where something is *situated*. When saying where things are, the verb **ficar** is used to refer to anything that has a fixed, permanent position, like a building, a garden, or a monument. Although **ficar** has other meanings, it is usually used to indicate location:

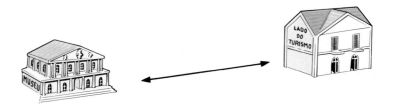

position
O museu fica ao lado do Turismo.   The museum is beside the Tourist Office.
location
A catedral fica na Praça da República.   The cathedral is in the Praça da Republica.
O hotel fica na rua Paraiso.   The hotel is in Paradise Street.
A estação fica na segunda rua à esquerda.   The station is in the second street on the left.

How to get there

Look at this phrase from the first dialogue: **tome a primeira (rua) à esquerda** (take the first (street) on the left). The verb **tomar** appears in the form of a *command* – **tome!** – known as the imperative. This form of the verb is used when giving directions, like this:

Siga em frente	Go straight on	**Corte** à esquerda	Turn left
Vire à direita	Turn right	**Vá** por aqui	Go this way

In, on, at

Em means 'in', 'on' or 'at'. When placed in front of a singular noun it combines with the **o** or the **a** which accompanies the noun to mean 'in the/at the', like this:

em + **o** = **no**   **em** + **o** banco = **no** banco   at the bank/in the bank.
em + **a** = **na**   **em** + **a** casa = **na** casa   in the house
note the exception: **em** casa (*at* home).

Similarly for the plural **os** and **as**:
em + **os** = **nos**   **em** + **os** carros = **nos** carros   in the cars
em + **as** = **nas**   **em** + **as** ruas = **nas** ruas   in the streets

Here are a few more examples of contraction of the article with a preposition:

de (of, from)	Lisboa é a capital **de** Portugal
	Lisbon is the capital of Portugal
de + o = do	Vinho **do** Porto (vinho de + o Porto)
	Port wine (lit. wine from o Porto)
de + a = da	Rua **da** Rosa (Rua de + a Rosa)
	Rose Street (lit. street of + the rose)
a + a = à	**à** esquerda/**à** direita
	on the left/on the right
a + o = ao	**ao** lado
	next to/beside the

Ter (to have)

When in the last dialogue José asked at the Tourist Office for a map, the verb he used was **ter** (to have):

Tem um mapa?	Do you have a map?
Sim, tenho.	Yes, I have.
Lamento, mas não tenho	Sorry (I regret) but I don't have (one).

Unlike English, **ter** doesn't need another verb and all you have to do to ask for something is to say '**tem**' followed by what you want:

Tem quartos vagos?
Tem gelado de chocolate?

Some of the uses of the verb **ter**:
1   to give the idea of having things for sale

Tem postais?   Do you have postcards?

2   to give the idea of having to do something

Tenho que ir   I have to go

3   to give the idea of availability, or of possessing (having) something

Tenho tempo   I have time
Tem dinheiro?   Do you have money?

4   to say how old you are

Quantos anos **tem?**   How old are you? (lit. how many years do you have?)
Tenho quinze anos   I am fifteen

5   to say that you are hungry or thirsty

Tenho fome e **tenho** sede   I'm hungry and thirsty

Here is the *present tense* of **ter**:

tenho	I have	**temos**	we have
tens	you have (familiar)	**tem**	they have
tem	you have	**tem**	you have (all)
tem	he/she/it has		

Instead of using the verb **ter**, you can say **há**, meaning 'there is', 'there are'/'is there?', 'are there?' (see Monday afternoon).

Verb groups

In Portuguese verbs can be grouped in three categories:

1st group   verbs ending in -**ar**, like fal**ar** (to speak), compr**ar** (to buy), cheg**ar** (to arrive)

2nd group   verbs ending in -**er**, like beb**er** (to drink), com**er** (to eat), t**er** (to have)

3rd group   verbs ending in -**ir**, like part**ir** (to leave).

So far you have met *irregular* verbs (**ser, estar, ter, querer**) i.e. the ones which do not follow a standard pattern when conjugated. Now for some easier ones, the *regular* ones. Here are two regular verbs of the same group, in the present tense:

	falar (to speak)	**chegar** (to arrive)
(I)	fal**o**	cheg**o**
(you)	fal**as**	cheg**as**
(he/she/it)	fal**a**	cheg**a**
(we)	fal**amos**	cheg**amos**
(you)	fal**am**	cheg**am**
(they)	fal**am**	cheg**am**

To conjugate *all* regular verbs of the -**ar** group, you just have to separate the root (e.g. **fal**, **cheg**) of the verb and add the same endings as above.

Now, let's have a look at some regular verbs of the *2nd* and *3rd groups* and their endings in the present tense:

	2nd group		*3rd group*
	beber (to drink)	**comer** (to eat)	**partir** (to leave)
(I)	beb**o**	com**o**	part**o**
(you)	beb**es**	com**es**	part**es**
(he/she/it)	beb**e**	com**e**	part**e**
(we)	beb**emos**	com**emos**	part**imos**
(you)	beb**em**	com**em**	part**em**
(they)	beb**em**	com**em**	part**em**

These are the same endings you will use for all the other regular verbs in these two groups.

19

things to do

2.1 Answer the questions using **ter** (to have):
1 Quantos anos tem?
(Say you are 20 or give your real age)
2 Tem filhos? Quantos?
(Say how many children you have. Remember: **não** in front of the verb if you haven't any)
3 Quantos quartos tem a sua casa?
(How many rooms does your house have?)

2.2 Look at the plan of central Lisbon. You are in the Praça do Comércio (on the spot marked * facing North) and you overhear these instructions being given to three passers-by. Where is each person going?

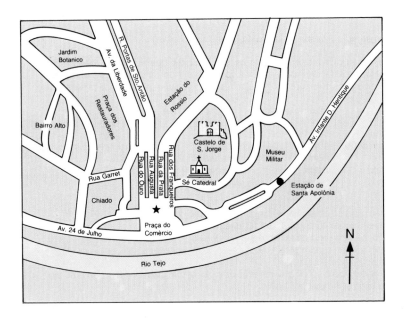

1a. pessoa: Corte a primeira à direita, siga em frente até o Museu Militar (a esquerda) e a . . . está à direita.

2a. pessoa: A senhora segue à direita e depois toma a segunda à direita. Continua em frente e a . . . está à esquerda.

3a. pessoa: Continua sempre em frente até o fim da Rua Augusta. Ali à direita está a . . .

FINDING OUT THE TIME

que horas são/what time is it?

The family is at the Rossio station to meet Cristina who is travelling from Beja.

Maria:	Frank, **que horas são?**
Frank:	**São dez e meia.**
Maria	(Maria goes up to the information desk) Faz favor, **à que horas parte** o comboio **de** Beja **para** Lisboa?
Funcionário:	**De manhã ou de tarde?**
Maria:	De manhã.
Funcionário:	Parte de Beja **às dez e um quarto.**
Maria:	E **à que horas chega** em Lisboa?
Funcionário:	Chega **às onze menos um quarto.**
Maria:	**Está à tabela?**
Funcionário:	O comboio que parte de Beja, **hoje** está **avariado. O próximo** comboio de Beja é amanhã de manhã.
Maria:	Oh! . . Obrigada. **Volto amanhã.**

Asking the time

Que horas são?	What time is it?
São dez (horas) e meia	It's half past ten
À que horas parte o comboio?	When/at what time does the train leave?

21

de Beja para Lisboa	from Beja to Lisbon
de manhã ou de tarde?	in the morning or in the afternoon?
parte às dez (horas) e um quarto	it leaves at a quarter past ten
À que horas chega?	When does it/he/she arrive?
Chega às onze (horas) menos um quarto	It arrives at a quarter to eleven
Está à tabela?	Is it on time?
Está atrasado/atrasada?	Is it late?
o comboio da manhã	the morning train
que parte/que chega	which leaves/arrives
está avariado	has broken down
volto mais tarde	I will come back later
volto dentro de meia hora	I'll come back within half an hour

Times of the day

de manhã	in the morning
de tarde	in the afternoon/early evening
de noite/à noite	in the evening/at night

Expressions of time

ontem/hoje/amanhã	yesterday/today/tomorrow
há uma hora/há uma semana atrás	an hour ago/a week ago
daqui a uma hora	an hour from now
dentro de meia hora	within half an hour
na próxima segunda feira	next Monday

For numbers, refer to the Topic Vocabulary at the back of the book.

the way it works

Understanding time

Que horas são? São . . .   What time is it? It is . . .

são duas (horas)   **são** seis (horas)   **são** nove (horas)

The verb **ser** is always used in the plural (**são**) except for one o'clock, midnight, and noon, and to say 'a quarter to' (**um quarto para**), when it is used in the singular (**é**):

é uma hora   it's one o'clock

é meio-dia   it's midday
é meia-noite   it's midnight

Os minutos (the minutes)

The word **e** (and) is used to 'add' the minute to the hour. The quarters of the hour are **um quarto**.

É uma (hora) **e** trinta (minutos)
É uma (hora) **e** meia

São duas (horas) **e** cinco (minutos)

São cinco (horas) **e** quinze (minutos)
São cinco (horas) **e** um quarto

The minutes *to the hour* are expressed either by the word **para** (to) or **menos** (less), like this:

São quinze (minutos) **para** as três (horas)
São três (horas) **menos** quinze (minutos)
São três (horas) **menos** um quarto
É um quarto **para** as três (horas)
or
São duas (horas) e quarenta e cinco (minutos)   (Two hours and forty-five minutes)

São doze (horas)
É meio-dia
É meia-noite

To say 'am' and 'pm'

am   São nove (horas) **da manhã**

pm   São três (horas) **da tarde**

São nove (horas) **da noite**   pm

To ask at what time something is happening, say . . .

À que horas. . .

  . . .parte   o comboio?
  . . .chega

at what time/when does. . .

  . . .the train   leave?
  arrive?

  . . .abre   o museu?
  . . .fecha

  . . .the museum   open?
  close?

From. . . . .to. . . . .
da. . . às. . .
das. . . às. . .   }   from. . . to. . .
das. . . ao. . .

Aberto
8.00 às
23.00
Horas

À que horas abre o museu?

O museu abre **da** uma (hora) **às** quatro (horas)

O museu abre **das** dez (horas) **às** duas (horas)

O museu abre **das** dez (horas) **ao** meio dia

When is the museum open?

The museum is open from one until four o'clock.

The museum is open from ten until two o'clock.

The museum is open from ten until midday.

Both the 12 hour and the 24 hour clock are used to tell the time, although the first is more common. Take some time to learn the numbers listed in the Vocabulary section at the back of the book, and you will find that telling and understanding the time in Portuguese will not present much difficulty. Official time in Portugal (transport, timetables, opening and closing times, etc) is calculated using the 24-hour clock. Here are some examples of the 24 hour clock:

13:50	São treze (horas) e cinquenta minutos	**20:00**	São vinte horas
14:00	O museu abre às catorze horas	**15:00**	O banco fecha às quinze horas

things to do

2.3   Can you tell the time? Write down the questions and the answers in Portuguese.

     e.g.   What time is it?   (9.15 am)
           Que horas são?   Sao nove e quinze da manhã.

1   At what time is breakfast served?   (from 8 to 10 am)
2   When does your friend arrive?   (7.15 am)
3   At what time does the train leave?   (15.30)
4   When does the museum open?   (9.45 am)

PUBLIC TRANSPORT

Transport   Portuguese railways provide an excellent network of services. Senior Citizens pay 50% of the fare, providing that a proof of age is submitted. The Inter-Rail ticket is valid in Portugal for those under 26 years of age. Children under 4 travel free, and from 4 to 12 pay half of the fare. Comfortable coach services also cover the country and timetables are available from local Tourist Offices and travel agencies in Portugal. The towns are all served by buses.

Bus services from Lisbon   The Portuguese Transport Company – **a Rodoviária Nacional (RN)** – serves most cities. Information about timetables (**o horário**) and terminals (**estações**), is obtainable from Tourist Offices. The Green Line (**a Linha Verde**) from Santa Apolonia railway station to Lisbon Airport operates daily with buses every 15 minutes. There are also buses to Faro, O Porto, Coimbra, etc.

Transport within Lisbon   Apart from the buses and taxis, Lisbon is served by trams (**o elétrico**), a very picturesque and popular form of transport, especially within the old part of the city (**o Bairro Alto**).

Tickets   Are very cheap, and even more so if bought in advance in blocks of 10 (each ticket worth two **módulos**) or of 20 (each worth one **módulo**) from any terminal station or ticket kiosk.

uma viagem de comboio/a train journey

Cristina is at the ticket office (**a bilheteria**) at Beja railway station. She is buying a ticket to Lisbon, and the clerk gives her the various possibilities.

Cristina:	Boa tarde. **Queria um bilhete** para Lisboa, por favor. Para hoje.
Funcionário:	**De ida** ou **de ida e volta?**
Cristina:	**Só de ida.**
Funcionário:	Está bem. A senhora **quer viajar no expresso** ou **no direto?**
Cristina:	**Quanto custa** o bilhete para o expresso?
Funcionário:	**Primeira classe** são mil e novecentos escudos, e de **segunda classe** são mil cento e cinquenta escudos.
Cristina:	**Fico com** o de segunda classe. Ah!... **não fumadores**, se faz favor.
Funcionário:	Sim senhora. Aqui está. **O comboio** parte **do cais número três, dentro de quinze minutos.**
Cristina:	Obrigada.

At the railway station

um bilhete	a ticket
só de ida	single only
de ida e volta	return
o comboio	the train
quer viajar . . .?	do you want to travel . . .?
no expresso	by express train
o direto	a through train
o rápido	a train which stops only at main stations
Quanto custa?	How much?
Quanto é?	How much?
primeira classe	first class
segunda classe	second class
fumadores/não fumadores	smokers/non smokers
um horário	the timetable
o cais número três	platform number three
dentro de quinze minutos	within fifteen minutes

Camionetas e comboios (Coaches and trains)

Onde é . . .?
o terminal das camionetas
a estação dos comboios
Qual é . . .?
o cais do comboio para . . .

Where is . . .?
the coach terminal
the railway station
Which is . . .?
the platform for the train to . . .

Autocarros e elétricos (Buses and trams)

These are your choices if you intend to go anywhere beyond easy walking distance within Lisbon. The fares are low and there is usually a service until midnight.

paragem de autocarros
Onde posso apanhar . . .?
o elétrico para . . .
um autocarro para . . .
Qual é o elétrico que vai
  para . . .?
Que autocarro devo
  apanhar para . . .?
Qual é o preço do
  bilhete?
Quanto custa o bilhete?/
Quanto é o bilhete?

bus stop
Where can I get . . .?
the tram to . . .
a bus to . . .
Which tram goes to . . .?

Which bus do I take for
  . . .?
What is the price of the
  ticket?
How much is the ticket?

The Lisbon underground has two main lines which join at Pombal Square. The price is the same for any distance, and the service stops at 1 am.

O Metrô (The underground)

Onde é/onde fica a estação do metrô?	Where is the underground station?
Que linha devo tomar para . . .?	Which line should I take for . . .?
É este o metrô para . . .?	Is this the train to . . .?
Onde é a máquina de venda de bilhetes?	Where is the ticket machine?

Taxis (táxis) are cheap and plentiful. Easily identified, Portuguese taxis are black with green roofs. They use meters and the basic fare includes the first 363 metres. After this you pay per km.

You can say: **Leve-me para. . . .**   Take me to. . . .
Or:
Para o museu Gulbenkian, por favor.
Para os Jerônimos, se faz favor.
And to ask how much, say: **Quanto é?**

AT THE BANK

The Portuguese currency unit is the **escudo**, which is made up of 100 **centavos**. One escudo is written 1$00. There are notes (**notas**) and coins (**moedas**). Notes are issued for 5.000$00, 1.000$00, 500$00, 100$00 and 50$00. Coins are issued for 50$00, 25$00, 20$00, 10$00, 5$00, 2$50, 1$00 and 00$50. 30$50 means thirty escudos and fifty cents.

You will need your passport for any transaction. You will be given a tag or a disc (**uma chapa**) with a number on it and asked to go to the cash desk (**a caixa**), to collect your money when it is your turn. International credit cards are widely accepted especially in the larger resorts. Banking hours are 8.30–11.45 and 13.00–14.45, Monday–Friday.

câmbio de dinheiro/money exchange

While Frank takes the children to the **Jardim Zoológico**, Maria makes her way to the bank to change some money.

Maria: Queria **trocar libras esterlinas**. À quanto está o câmbio hoje?

Funcionário: À duzentos e quarenta escudos (240$00). **Quantas** libras deseja trocar?

Maria: Cem libras.

Funcionário: O seu passaporte, por favor . . . **Quer assinar aqui?** Agora, **passe à caixa. Esta é a sua chapa.**

Bank language

dinheiro trocado	small change
notas/moedas	notes/coins
trocar	to change
libra esterlina	pound sterling
dólares	dollars
cheques de viagem	travellers' cheques
levantar um cheque	to cash a cheque
À como/À quanto está o câmbio?	What is the exchange rate?
Quanto/Quantos/Quantas?	How much?
Quer assinar aqui?	Would you sign here, please?
Passe à caixa	Go to the cashier
Esta é a sua chapa	This is your tag
Posso levantar dinheiro com este cartão de crédito?	Can I withdraw money with this credit card?

the way it works

I would like

Queria is the imperfect of the verb **querer** (to want) and it means 'would like':

(I)	quer**ia**	(we)	quer**íamos**
(you)	quer**ia**	(they)	quer**iam**
(he/she)	quer**ia**		

Queria um bilhete para hoje. I would like a ticket for today.
Queríamos comprar um horário. We would like to buy a timetable.

Fico com

Fico com is a useful Portuguese expression meaning 'I will take' when you have to choose between two or more options:

Fico com este. I will take this one.
Fico com o azul. I will take the blue one.
Fico com o bilhete de segunda classe. I will take the second class ticket.

things to do

3.1 You are at Sta. Apolónia station buying tickets to go to Coimbra with a friend for the day. How do you answer the clerk's questions?

Clerk: Para onde, se faz favor?
You: (You'd like 2 tickets to Coimbra, second class)
Clerk: Quando quer viajar?
You: (Say today, and that you want 2 returns)
Clerk: A senhora quer viajar no expresso ou no direto?
You: (Ask how much it is for 2nd class on the express)
Clerk: São mil e quatrocentos escudos.
You: (Ask for non-smoking seats; when does the train leave?)
Clerk: O comboio parte do cais número dois dentro de vinte minutos.
You: (Repeat what he said, but in the form of a question)

3.2 Maria is at the bank. Put the sentences below in the right order to make a dialogue.

1 O seu passaporte, por favor. Quanto quer trocar?
2 A quanto está o câmbio?
3· Aqui está a sua chapa. Quer passar à caixa?
4 Queria trocar libras esterlinas.
5 Vou trocar cem libras.
6 A duzentos e vinte escudos.
7 Sou eu. Aqui está.
8 Chapa número 34!

3.3 Write out the prices of these items in full:

BUYING POSTCARDS

vende postais?/do you sell postcards?

Célia and José want some postcards, so they stop at a news stand where they see some attractive ones.

Vendedora (to Célia):	**A menina** quer?
Célia:	Queria dois **postais**, faz favor.
Vendedora:	Pode escolher!
Célia:	**Estes** dois.
José:	Eu quero cinco, se faz favor. Dois **destes** e três **daqueles**.
Célia:	Quanto custam os postais?
Vendedora:	Sao dez escudos **cada um**.
José:	A senhora **tem selos**?
Vendedora:	Lamento, mas não tenho. **O menino** tem que **ir** ao correio.

The colourful **quiosques** (kiosks) on the pavements are part of the Portuguese street scene, selling anything from postcards to a variety of magazines and newspapers in many languages.

Queria . . .	I would like . . .
um postal de Lisboa	a postcard of Lisbon
uma revista Portuguesa	a Portuguese magazine
Vende . . .?	Do you sell . . .?
Há . . .?/Tem . . .?	Is/are there . . .?
journais Inglêses/Americanos	English/American newspapers
revistas em Inglês	magazines in English
Lamento mas não vendemos/temos . . .	I'm sorry but we don't sell/have . . .
Pode escolher	You can choose/please choose

no correio/at the post office

They go to the Post Office and Célia insists on buying the stamps for both of them. José is sending a postcard to his American friend, and Célia to friends in Spain and England.

Célia:	Boa tarde.
Funcionário:	Boa tarde. **A menina quer?**
Célia:	**Queria mandar** postais para a Inglaterra, os Estados Unidos e a Espanha. **Qual é o preço de cada** sêlo?
Funcionário:	Para a Inglaterra e Espanha, o sêlo custa vinte e cinco escudos. Para os Estados Unidos, trinta e cinco escudos.
Célia:	**Quero cinco sêlos** para Inglaterra, um para a Espanha e um para os Estados Unidos, por favor.
Funcionário:	**É tudo?**
Célia:	Sim, obrigada.

Post office

um sêlo	a stamp
Queria mandar/enviar . . .	I should like to send . . .
um postal	a postcard
uma carta	a letter
uma encomenda	a parcel
Quero cinco sêlos	I want five stamps
Quero mandar isto . . .	I want to send this . . .
por avião	by airmail
registado	by registered mail
É tudo?	Will that be all?

the way it works

How to address someone else's child

Portuguese people use **o menino** (young man) and **a menina** (young lady). They take the same 3rd person of the verb as **êle/ela**.

Some irregular plurals

Notice that, in the dialogue on page 31, the word **postal** (postcard), becomes **postais** in the plural. The plural of words ending in **-al**, **-el**, **-il**, **-ol** is irregular. Look how some of them change (there are exceptions):

singular		plural	
-al	o postal	**-ais**	os postais
-el	o papel	**-eis**	os papéis (the papers)
-il	o canil	**-is**	os canis (the kennels)
-ol	o caracól	**-ois**	os caracóis (the snails)

You will meet more irregular plurals – learn them as you go.

33

Can I choose, please?

Escolher is the verb 'to choose':
Pode escolher os postais.   (You) can choose the postcards.
Escolha!   Please choose!

This and that

If the object in question is close to the person you are speaking to, use **esse**, but if it is distant from both of the people who are talking, use **aquele**:

Masculine object		*Feminine object*	
this (car)	**esse** (carro)	this (street)	**essa** (rua)
that (car)	**aquele** (carro)	that (street)	**aquela** (rua)

Esse and **aquele** both have regular plurals

Of these, of those

In the previous chapter, you learned that **de** is one of the words for 'of'. When **de** combines with certain words, a new word is formed – a contraction.

before contraction	*becomes*	*plural*
de + este/esta	**deste/desta**	**destes/destas**
of + this	of this	of these
de + aquele/aquela	**daquele/daquela**	**daqueles/daquelas**
of + that	of that	of those

Ir (to go)

Tem que ir ao correio   You have to go to the Post Office.
The verb **ir** is irregular. Here is its present tense:

singular			*plural*		
eu	**vou**	(I go)	nós	**vamos**	(we go)
tu	**vais**	(you go)	vocês	**vão**	(you go)
você	**vai**	(you go)	êles/elas	**vão**	(they go)
êle/ela	**vai**	(he/she goes)			

The imperative (or command form) of **ir** is **vá!**:
Vá imediatamente!   Go at once!

things to do

3.4 Look at these pictures and using the verb **ir** (to go) write down where people are going:

1 Maria . . . para . . .
2 Célia e José . . . ao . . .
3 Nós . . . ao . . .
4 Eu . . . para o . . .

GOING SHOPPING

▶ **Shopping and business hours**   Shops are usually open from 09.00 to 13.00 and 15.00 to 19.00, Monday–Friday. On Saturdays they are open from 09.00 to 13.00. Credit cards are acceptable nearly everywhere.

a sapataria/the shoe shop

Maria wants to buy herself some summer sandals in an elegant shop in the fashionable Chiado shopping area. She looks around the shelves in the shop and the salesgirl comes up.

Girl: **Em que posso servi-la?**
Maria: **Posso ver** as sandálias de verão, por favor?
Girl: **Que número calça** a senhora?
Maria: Trinta e oito.
Girl: Em que côr quer as sandálias?
Maria: Queria brancas de salto raso. **Posso provar várias?**
Girl: **Com certeza. Vou trazer-lhe** dois ou três pares.
Maria: (after trying them on) **Aquelas** sandálias **não ficam bem apertam-me os pés. Estas ficam melhor** e são elegantes. **Gosto muito**. Qual é o preço?
Girl: Três mil escudos.
Maria: **Fico com elas. Posso pagar com cartão de crédito?**
Girl: **Não há problema. Quer passar à caixa,** se faz favor?

35

At the shoe shop

Posso ver . . .?	Can I see . . .?
sandálias de verão	summer sandals
número trinta e oito	size 38
brancas de salto raso	white with flat heels
Posso provar várias?	May I try several (pairs) on?
com certeza	certainly
um par/dois pares	one pair/two pairs
não ficam bem	don't fit well
apertam-me os pés	they pinch my feet
ficam melhor	these fit better
Gosto muito	I like (it/them) very much
Fico com elas	I'll take them
Posso pagar . . .?	Can I pay . . .?
Não há problema	There is no problem/certainly

Vestuário e calçados (Clothing and shoes)

The questions you are asked

Em que posso servi-la (lo)?	Can I help you?
Quer ajuda?	Can I help you?
Que número calça?	What size (shoe) do you take?
Que número veste?	What size (of clothes) are you?
Que tamanho?	What size?
Em que côr/Qual é a cor?	In which colour?/Which colour?
Salto alto?/Salto raso?	High heels?/Flat heels?
Gosta deste/desta?	Do you like this one?
Mais alguma coisa?	Anything else?
Quer maior?/menor?	Do you want a larger size?/a smaller size?
É tudo?/É só?	Is that all?

The questions you ask

Posso ver . . .?	May I have a look at . . .?
Posso experimentá-la(lo)?	May I try it on?
Tem noutra côr?	Do you have it in another colour?
Tem noutro tecido?	Do you have it in another fabric?
Tem noutro modelo?	Do you have it in another style?
Tem mais barato?	Do you have a cheaper one?
Tem maior?	Do you have it in a larger size?
Tem menor?	Do you have it in a smaller size?
Tem mais curto/mais comprido?	Do you have a shorter/longer one?
Tem mais grosso/mais fino?	Do you have a thicker/thinner one?
É cabedal (or couro) genuino?	Is it real leather?

Useful phrases

Não gosto	I don't like it
Não me serve	It doesn't fit me
É caro demais	It's too expensive
Não é *bem* o que quero	It's not quite what I want
Prefiro êste/aquele	I prefer this/that one
o da vitrine	the one in the shop window
Só estou olhando	I am just looking
o vestido/a saia	dress/skirt
LIQUIDAÇÕES/SALDOS	SALE/BARGAINS

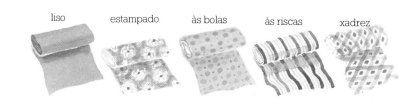

liso	estampado	às bolas	às riscas	xadrez

Tipos de tecido (Types of fabric)

linho	linen	lã	wool
poliester	polyester	popelina	poplin
veludo	velvet	seda	silk
algodão	cotton	cetim	satin

Look out for these signs:

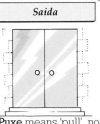
Saída

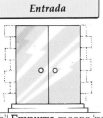
Entrada

Saída de emergência

Puxe means 'pull', not 'push'! **Empurre** means 'push'.

Sizes

Medidas de senhora (Women's sizes)

	Clothes						Shoes			
British	10	12	14	16	18	20	3	4	5	6
Portuguese	38	40	42	44	46	48	36	37	38	39
American	8	10	12	14	16	18	4½	5½	6½	7½

Medidas de homen (Men's sizes)

Shirts

British	14	14½	15	15½	16	16½	17
Portuguese	36	37	38	39	41	42	43
American	14	14½	15	15½	16	16½	17

Shoes

British	5	6	7	8	9	10
Portuguese	37½	39	40½	41½	42½	44
American	5	6	7	8	8½	9

SHOPPING FOR FOOD

Food is sold by **quilo** (kilo), **gramas** (grams), **pacotes** (packets), **latas** (tins), and **litros** (litres).

Remember that it is: **um** grama; **um** quilo; **uma** dúzia; **um** litro; **um** pacote; **uma** lata.

100 g = 3.5 oz	1 oz = 28.35 g
250 g = 8.75 oz	1 lb = 453.60 g
½ kg = 1.1 lb	1 kg = 2.2 lb

The food shops

o talho	the butcher's
a peixaria	the fishmonger's
a loja de verduras	the greengrocer's
a mercearia	the grocery shop
o mercado	the market
o supermercado	the supermarket

To ask for what you want, say: **Me dê . . .; Queria . . .; Tem . . .?**

Me dê duzentos gramas daquele presunto.   Give me 200 g of that ham.
Queria um pacote de biscoitos.   I'd like a packet of biscuits.
Tem vinho branco?   Do you have white wine?

38

Uma lista de compras (A shopping list)

meia dúzia/uma dúzia de ovos	half dozen/a dozen eggs
um litro de leite	a litre of milk
cem gramas de presunto	100 g ham
cem gramas de queijo	100 g cheese
meio quilo de tomates	½ kilo of tomatoes
um quilo e meio de peixe	1½ kilo of fish
um quilo de carne	1 kilo of meat
dois quilos de batatas	2 kilos of potatoes
um pacote de biscoitos	a packet of biscuits
uma lata de azeite	a can of oil
duzentos gramas de toucinho	200 g bacon

the way it works

May I?/Can I?

Look at the word **posso** in the last dialogue: **Posso ver? Posso provar? Posso pagar? Posso?** means 'Can I?' It comes from the verb **poder** (to be able to, can). This is its present tense:

singular		*plural*	
posso	I can	**podemos**	we can
podes	you can	**podem**	you can
pode	you can	**podem**	they can
pode	he/she/it can		

You will often see this verb used with the impersonal pronoun **se** (one/you) in public notices like:

Não se pode estacionar	Parking not allowed
Não se pode fumar	No smoking
Não se pode tocar	Don't touch

Object pronouns (me, her, etc.)

This is a complex aspect of Portuguese grammar, and cannot be covered fully in this book. Here however is a brief guide:

Pronouns	I, you, she ...	eu	tu	êle/ela	nós	vocês	êles/elas
Reflexive pronouns	myself, yourself ...	me	te	se	nos	se	se
Indirect object	me, you, him, her, us, you, them	me	te	lhe	nos	lhes	lhes
Direct object		me	te	o/a	nos	os/as	os/as

Reflexive
Lavo-me diáriamente.
Ela **chama-se** Maria.

I wash *myself* every day.
She is called (calls *herself*) Maria.

Indirect
Estas sandálias **apertam-me** os pés.
Comprei-lhe um presente.

(see the dialogue on page 35)
I bought *him/her* a present.

Direct
Ele **levou-a** à sapataria.
Onde estão as crianças? Não **as vejo.**

He took *her* to the shoe shop.
Where are the children? I don't see *them.*

I like it, I don't like it

Here is the verb **gostar** (to like), in the present tense:

gosto	I like	**gostamos**	we like
gostas	you like	**gostam**	you like
gosta	you like	**gostam**	they like
gosta	he/she it likes		

Remember that to make a negative statement you just need to put **não** before the verb: **Não gosto.**

A **?** is all you need to transform a statement into a question: **Gostas?** Do you like?

Cheap, cheaper

Mais means 'more', so **mais barato** literally means 'more cheap' = 'cheaper', and **mais caro** = 'more expensive'. You can apply this to other adjectives:

mais caro	dearer	**mais curto**	shorter
mais largo	wider	**mais apertado**	tighter

But you will come across exceptions like:

menor	smaller	**melhor**	better/best
maior	bigger	**pior**	worse/worst

To *compare* two things, say **mais . . . que**; **menor . . . que** etc. To say 'it is *the* best', etc, just put **o/a** before the adjective: este hotel é **o melhor/o mais caro.**

Saying what you are going to do in the future

The immediate future tense is formed by the present tense of **ir** (to go), followed by an infinitive.

Vou	**trazer**	dois ou três pares.
present of **ir**	+ *to bring*	
I am going	to bring	two or three pairs.

Eu vou levar	I am going to take
Tu vais ver	You are going to see
Êle vai partir	He is going to leave

things to do

1 Write down what each person below wants to buy:

1	Cristina quer . . .	4	Maria . . .
2	Célia quer comprar	5	Sra. Gomes . . .
3	Frank queria		

2 Where will each of these people have to go to buy what they want? Use **à**, **ao**, **no**, **na**. (See list of shops on pages 87 and 89)
1 Cristina vai . . .
2 Célia vai comprar . . . no . . .
3 Frank vai . . .
4 Maria vai comprar . . .
5 Sra. Gomes vai . . . e . . .

3 You are self-catering and you need these items. There is no supermarket so you have to ask for them in the **mercearia**:

4 Using the verb **gostar** answer these questions according to the clue given:

E.g: Do you like wine?   (*)   Yes, we do.
Do they like music?   (**)   Yes, they like it very much.
Do you like the house?   (***)   No, I don't like it.

1 Eles gostam de frutos do mar?   (*)
2 Gosta deste tecido?   (***)
3 Sua mulher gosta de seda?   (**)
4 Os senhores gostam do hotel?   (*)

A PHONE CALL

quem fala?/who's speaking?

Back at her hotel room, Maria answers the phone.

Maria:	**Está? Quem fala?**
Voice:	**Aqui fala** tua mãe, Maria. Como estão todos?
Maria:	Muito bem, mãe. Vamos à Sintra amanhã de manhã. ĩã. Està bem?
Sra. Gomes:	**Pois!** Gostaria muito de vê-los.
Maria:	**Vamos chegar aí** às dez horas, **mais ou menos.**
Sra. Gomes:	Até amanhã, **então.**
Maria:	Adeus, mãe e até amanhã.

Speaking on the phone

Está?/Estou?	Hello
Quem fala?	Who is speaking?
Aqui fala (tua mãe)	This is (your mother) speaking
Queria falar com . . .	I'd like to speak to . . .
Pode falar mais devagar.	Speak more slowly, please.
Um momento, não desligue!	Just a moment, don't hang up!
Volto a chamar mais tarde	I'll call again later

Understanding the replies

(o senhor/a senhora) ligou o número errado	you have dialled the wrong number
(êle/ela) saiu/não está	(he/she) is out/isn't here
está de férias	is on holiday
está numa reunião	is at a meeting
não vem hoje	will not be here (come) today
Quer deixar um recado?	Do you want to leave a message?
Um momento, por favor	Hold the line, please

Telephone words

o telefone	telephone
a telefonista	operator
a lista telefónica	telephone directory
a cabine telefónica	telephone booth

Asking for help

Telefonista, pode ajudar-me a ligar para este número?	Operator, could you help me to get this number?
Quero ligar para a Inglaterra, número . . ./Quero fazer uma chamada para . . .	I want to make a call to England, number . . . . .
Quero uma chamada à cobrar no destino	I want to reverse the charges
Cortaram-me a ligação!	I have been cut off!

SIGHTSEEING

vamos visitar o castelo/let's visit the castle

Frank is taking the children to see the touristic and historical attractions of Lisbon, so he asks for some leaflets at the hotel reception.

Frank:	Tem **algum folheto** com os pontos turísticos de Lisboa?
Recepcionista:	Sim, tenho **alguns**. Aqui estão.
Frank:	(to the children) Bem, **já conhecemos** o Jardim Zoológico. **Vamos visitar** o Mosteiro dos Jerônimos e a Tôrre de Belém. **Que acham**?
José e Célia:	Está bem.

43

Tem *algum* folheto?	Do you have *any/some* leaflets?
Sim, tenho alguns	Yes, I have some
os pontos turísticos	the touristic attractions
Já conhecemos . . .	We already know . . .
Que acha/acham?	What do you think?
Está bem.	It's alright/OK.

Vamos visitar (Let's visit . . .)

a catedral/a igreja/o castelo	the cathedral/the church/the castle
o Mosteiro dos Jerónimos	the Jeronimos Monastery
os jardins/os parques/o museu	the gardens/the parks/the museum
o centro/a parte velha (antiga) da cidade	the city centre/the old town

Admission

À que horas abre/fecha . . .?	When does . . . open/close?
Quanto custa a entrada?	How much is the admission fee?
Há desconto para crianças/estudantes/ aposentados?	Is there a reduction for children/ students/retired people?

the way it works

Pois

Although **pois** means 'because', 'then', 'so', or 'since', it is also much used in Portuguese as a term of agreement, to say 'yes, of course,' etc . . .

Vou visitá-la amanhã.	I will visit you tomorrow
Pois. Vou esperá-la.	Yes/OK, I'll wait for you.
Posso vê-la amanhã?	Can I see you tomorrow?
Pois claro (que não)!	Certainly (not)!

Here and there

here:	aqui	*there:*	lá
	cá		ali (nearer than **lá**)
			aí (near the person you are talking to)

Some, any

In the dialogue on page 43, Frank asks for **algum folheto** (any leaflets). **Algum** means either 'any' or 'some'. It agrees in both number and gender with the word it accompanies, e.g:

o folheto   alg**um** folheto; **a** lista telefônica   alg**uma** lista telefônica
os folhet**os**   alg**uns** folhet**os**; **as** lista**s** telefônica**s**   alg**umas** lista**s** telefônica**s**

Already, not yet

já   already   **já não**   no longer   **ainda**   still   **ainda não**   not yet

Já vou.   I am going *now*
Já conhecemos este museu   We *already know* this museum.

Q   **Já** conhecem a Catedral?   *Do you know* the Cathedral?
A   Sim, **já.**   Yes, we know (*already*) the Cathedral
       Não, **ainda não.**   No, *not yet* or No, we *still* don't.

Q   **Ainda** estão em Lisboa?   Are you *still* in Lisbon?
A   Sim, **ainda** estamos.   Yes, we *still* are.
       Não, **já não** estamos.   No, we are *no longer* in Lisbon.

things to do

4.5   How do you say . . .?
    1   Operator, I want to call England,
    2   number 801526.
    3   Reverse the charges, please.

4.6   Choose the Portuguese corresponding to 'already', 'not yet', 'still' from the list
    below, and complete the phrases:
    ainda   **ainda não**   **já**
    1   Have you ever been to Portugal?
         (Sim, .../Não, ...)
    2   Are they still here?
         (Sim, ...)
    3   Have they already packed?
         (Sim, ...)
    4   Have you (*pl.*) packed yet?
         (Não, ...)

A VISIT TO THE DOCTOR

British visitors to Portugal should read DHSS leaflets SA40 and SA41 and obtain the certificate E111 from their local DHSS office. On production of this certificate with your British passport, you are entitled to emergency medical treatment in Portugal, under the EEC Social Security regulations. There is a British Hospital at 49, Rua Saraiva de Carvalho, Lisbon.

não me sinto bem/I don't feel well

The Evans are visiting Maria's mother and sister Isabel in Sintra. Célia is not feeling well and Maria takes her to see a doctor.

Médico: (to Maria) Qual é o problema, minha senhora?
Maria: Eu estou bem, **doutor**. É a minha filha que **se sente mal**.
Médico: (to Célia) **O que sente** a menina?
Célia: **Dói-me** aqui (pointing to her stomach).
Maria: Ela **vomitou** esta manhã e **tem diarréia**.
Médico: Uhm . . . Quando começou a **sentir-se mal**?
Maria: Hoje cedo.
Médico: (to Célia) **Vou examiná-la. Deite-se aqui**, se faz favor. **Dói-lhe a cabeça?**
Célia: Um pouco.
Maria: **Acho que** ela comeu alguma coisa que lhe fêz mal.
Médico: A senhora está certa. Ela tem **uma indigestão. Aconselho uma dieta leve** e **vou receitar-lhe um medicamento**. Dê-lhe um comprimido duas vêzes por dia. Ela vai melhorar logo.
Maria: Muito obrigada, doutor.
Médico: De nada. Adeus.

No consultório médico (In the doctor's surgery)

Qual é o problema?	What's the matter?
Não me sinto bem.	I don't feel well
Ela se sente mal	She feels ill
O que sente?	What do you feel?
Dói-me o estômago	I have a pain in my stomach
Dói-lhe a cabeça/Tem dôr de cabeça?	Do you have a headache?
Eu vomitei/ela vomitou	I have/she has been vomiting
Ela tem diarréia	She has diarrhoea
Quando começou a sentir-se mal?	When did you/she begin to feel unwell?
Vou examiná-la(lo)	I am going to examine you
Deite-se aqui, por favor	Lie down over here, please
Acho que . . .	I think that . . .
ela comeu alguma coisa	she ate something
que lhe fêz mal	that made her ill
a senhora está certa	you are right
Ela tem uma indigestão	she has a stomach upset
uma leve intoxicação alimentar	food poisoning (not serious)
Aconselho. . . .	I advise. . . .
um dieta leve	a light diet
repouso	some rest
Vou receitar-lhe/ recomendo	I am going to prescribe/I recommend
este medicamento	this medicine
Tome/dê-lhe um comprimido	Take/give her/him one tablet
duas vêzes por dia	twice a day
Ela vai melhorar	She will get better

Seeking medical help

Estou doente	I am ill
Preciso de um médico, depressa	I need a doctor, quickly
Tenho uma dôr no/na . . .	I have a pain in my . . .
Onde é o hospital mais próximo?	Where is the nearest hospital?
Há um consultório médico perto daqui?	Is there a doctor's surgery nearby?
Queria marcar uma consulta	I'd like to make an appointment

A farmácia (The chemist)

drogaria	drugstore
farmácia de plantão	duty chemist
Tem este medicamento?	Do you have this medicine?
soro fisiológico para lentes de contacto?	cleaning solution for contact lenses
comprimidos para dôr de cabeça?	headache tablets?

O dentista (The dentist)

Pode recomendar-me um bom dentista?	Can you recommend a good dentist?
Tenho uma dor de dentes	I have toothache
dói-me este dente	this tooth aches
A gengiva sangra/dói	the gum is bleeding/sore
Êste dente/a minha dentadura partiu-se	this tooth/my denture is broken

Useful phrases and expressions

Queimadura de sol	sunburn
Insolação	sunstroke
Tenho febre	I have a fever
Sou alérgico(a) à . . .	I am allergic to . . .
Sou diabético(a)	I am diabetic
Pode dar-me um recibo para o meu seguro de saúde?	Can you give me a receipt for my health insurance?

CAMPING PLANS

Portuguese camp sites range from the basic to the most complete and well equipped sites. You will need your passport, and some sites will require the membership card of a camping association.

pode-se acampar aqui?/can we camp here?

Cristina and Isabel are going camping in the Algarve. They discuss their plans.

Isabel:	**Está tudo arranjado**, Cristina. **Temos um lugar reservado** no **parque de campismo** 'Campos Verdes'. É um Parque moderno e bem equipado. **Há** um restaurante, lojas, lavandaria, àgua quente e eletricidade.
Cristina:	Que bom! Vamos levar a minha tenda ou a tua?
Isabel:	A minha, pois é a maior, não acha?
Cristina:	Sim. Partimos hoje à tarde, então?
Isabel:	Sim. Algarve, aqui vamos nós!

Está tudo arranjado	It's all arranged
temos um lugar reservado	we have a place reserved
o parque de campismo	the camp site
moderno e bem equipado	modern and well equipped
Há um restaurante/lojas/lavandaria/ àgua quente/eletricidade	There is a restaurant/shops/a laundry/ hot water/electricity
Vamos levar a tenda maior	Let's take the bigger tent
Algarve, aqui vamos nós!	Algarve, here we go!

Booking a camp site

Há aqui um parque de campismo?	Is there a camp site here?
Há lugares para acampar?	Are there places to camp?
com tenda/caravana	with tent/caravan
Pode-se acampar aqui?	Can we camp here?
Há chuveiro/ducha?	Is there a shower?
àgua potável?	drinking water?
àgua quente?	hot water?
um armazém?	a grocery shop?
Onde é/fica a gerência?	Where is the management office?
o restaurante/a cafeteria	the restaurant/snack-bar
Onde ficam os chuveiros?	Where are the showers?
Há aqui um campo de ténis/uma piscina?	Is there a tennis court/a swimming pool here?
Pode-se alugar raquetes?	Can one hire tennis rackets?
Pode-se estacionar aqui?	Can one park here?

the way it works

Reflexive verbs

A verb in the reflexive form takes a **-se**, like **chamar-se** (to be called) or **vestir-se** (to dress oneself). It refers to actions done by oneself to oneself. The reflexive verbs are used with the reflexive pronouns given on page 39.

sentir-**se** mal	to feel unwell (ill)
A minha filha sente-**se** mal	My daughter is feeling unwell

deitar-**se**	to lie down
Vou deitar-**me** cedo hoje	I'm going to bed early today

chamar-**se**	to be called
Ela chama-**se** Célia	Her name is (she is called) Célia

Fala-**se** inglês	English is spoken here
Vende-**se** esta casa	This house is for sale
Pode-**se** estacionar aqui?	Can one park here?

SEXTA-FEIRA FRIDAY

Expressing your opinion (I think that . . .)

To express your opinion, use the verbs **achar** (to find) or **pensar** (to think) followed by **que**:

Acho que ela está doente	I think that she is ill
Penso que êle está doente	I think that she is ill
Acho que sim	I think so
Acho que não	I don't think so

How to say what happened in the past

Here is the preterite (past tense) for each of the three kinds of regular verb (**-ar**, **-er** and **-ir**). These endings are the same for all regular verbs.

	gostar (to like)	**correr** (to run)	**sair** (to go out)
eu	gost**ei**	corr**i**	sa**i**
tu	gost**astes**	corr**estes**	sa**istes**
você, etc	gost**ou**	corr**eu**	sa**iu**
êle/ela	gost**ou**	corr**eu**	sa**iu**
nós	gost**amos**	corr**emos**	sa**imos**
vocês, etc	gost**aram**	corr**eram**	sa**iram**
êles/elas	gost**aram**	corr**eram**	sa**iram**

things to do

5.1 You wake up with stomach ache. You go to the chemist for advice.

You:	(Greet him and say you have a pain in your stomach and ask if he can recommend something)
Chemist:	Quando começou a sentir-se mal?
You:	(Say 'this morning'. Perhaps you ate something that disagreed with you)
Chemist:	Acho que tem uma indigestão.
You:	(Ask him what is his advice)
Chemist:	Vou dar-lhe uns comprimidos.
You:	(Ask him how many you should take and how many times a day).
Chemist:	Tome um comprimido três vêzes por dia.

5.2 In the dialogue above, what was:
1 The question the chemist asked you?
2 His opinion about the nature of your complaint?
3 The medicine he prescribed and his instructions about how to take it?

5.3 How do you say the following?

1 My head aches
2 This tooth hurts
3 Can you recommend a doctor?
4 I vomited
5 I don't feel well
6 Where is there a chemist?
7 I am ill/sick

5.4 Each one of these people has some kind of ache or pain. Complete the phrases according to the pictures (use the Topic Vocabulary if necessary):

1 Maria tem uma dôr . . .
2 José tem uma dôr . . .
3 Frank tem uma dôr . . .
4 Cristina tem uma dôr . . .

5.5 In this picture, Melhoral, a popular medicine obtainable from chemists, is advertised. Can you tell what it's for?

Melhoral

dores de cabeça
febre
constipações
gripe

FARMÁCIA

PINHEIRO

DRIVING AND BREAKDOWNS

▶ **Rules of the road** · Portugal uses the international road sign system. The rule of the road is to keep to the *right* and overtake on the *left*. Traffic approaching from the *right* must be given priority, except when entering a public road from a private driveway or a side road with the STOP sign. At roundabouts, crossroads and junctions, traffic approaching from the *right* has priority. The major roads are signposted **N** with a number.

Speed Limits for cars: in built up areas: 60 kph (37 mph)
outside towns : 90 kph (55 mph)
on motorways : min. 40 kph (26 mph)
max. 120 kph (75 mph)

A British driving licence – **a carta de condução** – is valid. A GB sticker is compulsory for British cars, and seat belts should be worn. Petrol (**a gasolina**) is sold in litres (1 gallon = approx. 4.5 litres) and is available in two grades: **super** (4 star) and **normal** (2 star). Petrol stations (**a estação de serviço**) are usually open from 8.00 am to 12.00 noon and from 2.00 pm to 7.00 pm. They are very infrequent away from the bigger towns so make sure you have enough petrol before leaving the main roads.

53

Na estação de serviço (At the petrol station)

Meta dez litros de super, se faz favor	Put in 10 litres of 4 star, please
Encha o depósito, por favor	Fill it up, please
Pode verificar . . .?	Could you check . . .?
o óleo/a àgua	the oil/the water
a pressão dos pneus	the tyre pressure
a bateria	the battery
Há uma garagem perto daqui?	Is there a garage nearby?

uma avaria/a breakdown

Cristina and Isabel have problems with their car on the way to the Algarve. They stop at a garage recommended by the petrol station assistant.

Isabel:	Faz favor . . . (mechanic approaches) **meu carro está avariado**. Pode verificar?
Mecânico:	Qual é o problema?
Isabel:	Acho que há **um defeito no radiador. O motor aquece** demais.
Mecânico:	Vamos ver . . . a senhora está com sorte. O defeito não é no radiador, **é só uma fuga** na mangueira. Vou trocá-la.
Isabel:	**Vai demorar?**
Mecânico:	Não, é um serviço rápido.

Meu carro está avariado	My car has broken down
Pode verificar?	Can you have a look?
Acho que há um defeito no . . .	I think that . . . is faulty
o radiador	the radiator
os travões	the brakes
a ignição	the ignition
numa roda	a wheel
o motor aquece demais	the engine is overheating
o motor não pega	the engine won't start
o pneu está furado	the tyre has a puncture
o pneu está vazio	the tyre is flat
Vamos ver	Let's see
está com sorte	you are lucky
É só uma fuga na mangueira	It's only a leak in the hose
Vou trocá-la	I will change it
Vai demorar?	Will it take long?
Não, é um serviço rápido	No, it's a quick job
Sim, é um serviço demorado	Yes, it's a long job
Quanto lhe devo?	How much do I owe you?

Sinais de trânsito (Road signs)

CUIDADO!	CAUTION!
DEVAGAR!	SLOW!
ESTACIONAMENTO	CAR PARK
ESTACIONAMENTO PROIBIDO	NO PARKING
PARE!	STOP!
PEÕES	PEDESTRIANS
PASSAGEM DE PEÕES	PEDESTRIAN CROSSING
PERIGO	DANGER
PORTAGEM	TOLL
SEM SAIDA	NO THOUGH ROAD
SEMÁFOROS	TRAFFIC LIGHTS
TRÂNSITO PROIBIDO	NO TRAFFIC
TROÇO	STRETCH (of road)
TROÇO EM OBRAS	ROAD WORKS

things to do

6.6 You need to stop at a garage. How do you say:
1. My car has broken down. Can you have a look at it?
2. I have a flat tyre.
3. Could you check the oil and water, please?
4. The engine is overheating.

6.7 You are driving along and you see these road signs. What do they mean?
1. PERIGO! PARE!
2. CUIDADO! PASSAGEM DE PEÕES!
3. PORTAGEM À 500 metros
4. TRÂNSITO PROIBIDO

AT THE SEASIDE

na praia/on the beach

It's a sunny Saturday: Maria and Frank take the children to one of the beaches near Sintra.

Frank: **Pode-se nadar** sem perigo nesta praia, Maria?
Maria: **Pois!** O mar aqui é calmo.
Frank: Não há correntes perigosas?
Maria: Penso que não, mas gosto de ver as crianças banhar-se na beira da àgua.
Célia: José, **onde estão** as pranchas?
José: **Eu não sei**. Não estão no carro.
Célia: Ah! José esqueceu as pranchas. Que cabeça de vento!

a praia	the beach
Pode-se nadar sem perigo?	Can we swim safely?
Pois! O mar aqui é calmo	Of course! The sea is calm here
correntes perigosas	dangerous currents
Gosto de ver as crianças . . .	I like to see the children . . .
banhar-se na beira da àgua	bathing on the shore
Onde estão as pranchas?	Where are the surfboards?
Eu não sei	I don't know
Não estão no carro	They are not in the car
José esqueceu as pranchas	José forgot the surfboards
Que cabeça de vento!	What a scatter brain!

o almoço/lunch

It's lunch time and they have to go back home. Maria calls the children.

Maria: Célia, José! É hora do almoço. Venham secar-se, vestir-se e pentear-se. **Temos que voltar para casa.**

José: Ah, mãe! . . . Vamos ficar **até mais tarde** . . . Não se quer bronzear um pouco mais?

Maria: És muito vivo, José . . . mas não quero bronzear-me mais. Por hoje, chega.

Célia: **Que pena!** Eu queria ficar um pouco mais!

Frank: Eu também. O sol está uma beleza, mas a vovó espera nos para almoçar.

o almoço	lunch
almoçar	to have lunch
É a hora do almoço	It's lunch time
secar-se/vestir-se	to dry oneself/to dress (oneself)
pentear-se	to comb (one's hair)
bronzear-se	to sunbathe (to tan)
Temos que voltar para casa	We have to go back home
ficar até mais tarde	to stay until later
um pouco mais	a little more/a little longer
eu também	me too
O sol/a praia está uma beleza	The sun/the beach is lovely
a vovó/o vovô . . .	grandmother/grandfather . . .
espera-nos (me, o, a, etc)	is expecting/waiting for us (me, you, etc)

Useful phrases and expressions

És muito vivo (viva)!	You are very smart!
Por hoje chega!	That's enough for today!
Que pena!	What a pity!
Que beleza!	How beautiful!
Uma beleza!	beautiful! lovely! great!
Que dia mais belo/lindo!	What a lovely day!

Na praia (On the beach)

as ondas/a areia/a àgua	the waves/the sand/the water
o parasol/a bóia	the beach umbrella/the life buoy

o barco à vela	the sailing boat
a prancha à vela	the sail board
o banheiro	the lifeguard

DESCRIBING THE DAY

gostaram da praia?/did you like the beach?

Back in Sintra, grandmother wants to know what the morning on the beach was like.

Sra. Gomes:	Gostaram da praia? Como estava **o tempo**?
Célia::	Eu gostei muito. Eu e José encontramos muitas conchinhas.
José:	O sol estava forte e não havia vento.
Maria:	É verdade. **Estava** mesmo **quente demais**. Saimos da praia na hora certa!
Sra. Gomes:	Vejo que estão com uma côr saudável! O ar do mar sempre faz bem.

o tempo	the weather
Encontramos muitas (muitos) conchinhas	We found a lot of little shells
O sol estava forte/quente	The sun was strong/hot
Não tinha vento	There was no wind
Estava quente demais	It was too hot
Saimos na hora certa	We left at the right time
Vejo que . . .	I can see that . . .
estão com uma côr saudável	you have a healthy (skin) colour
o ar do mar	the sea air
faz bem/faz mal (não faz bem)	does you good/doesn't do you good

the way it works

More reflexive verbs

Banhar-se (-me, etc.)	to bathe/to have a bath
Vou banhar-**me** mais tarde	I'll have a bath later
Bronzear-se	to tan/to sunbathe
Bronzeio-**me** facilmente	I tan easily
Pentear-se	to comb (one's hair)
Célia, vai pentear-**te**!	Célia, go and comb your hair!
Secar-se	to dry oneself
Crianças, venham secar-**se**!	Children, come and dry yourselves!
Vestir-se	to get dressed/to dress up
Ela veste-**se** bem	She dresses (herself) well

Describing places and things

To describe things, people, events, etc. in the past, use the irregular verbs **ser** and **estar** (both meaning *to be*) in the imperfect indicative. Use **ser** to describe what people, things, etc. looked like and behaved like, and **estar** to say what people were doing or wearing, or how the weather was.

I was	you were	she/he/it was	we were	you were	they were
era estava	eras estavas	era estava	erámos estávamos	eram estavam	

Ela **era** morena e alta	She was dark and tall
A areia **era** macia	The sand was soft
Ela **estava** a bronzear-se	She was sunbathing
O tempo **estava** bom	The weather was good

Talking about the weather

A previsão do tempo	The weather forecast
Que dia lindo!	What a lovely day!
Que dia/tempo horrível!	What an awful day/weather
Faz calor/frio hoje!	It's hot/cold today!
o aguaceiro	shower

nouns		*adjectives*	
o sol	the sun	**ensolarado**	sunny
a chuva	the rain	**chuvoso**	rainy
o vento	the wind	**ventoso**	windy
a nuvem	the cloud	**nublado**	cloudy
o frio	the cold	**quente/calor**	hot
o calor	the heat	**frio**	cold

Note: **Frio** and **calor** can be both adjective and noun.

Ter or **estar com** are used to say whether people are hot or cold, hungry or thirsty, e.g:

Tenho/temos/tem frio/fome	I am/we/they are cold/hungry
Estou (etc) **com** calor/sede	I am (etc) hot/warm/thirsty

Estar and fazer
Use **estar** with an *adjective*, e.g: **Esta/estava** quente   It is/was hot/warm

Use **fazer** with a *noun*. **Há** (there is) and **havia** (there was) are also used for weather, applied in the same way as **fazer**:
Faz/Há muito sol no Algarve. **Fazia/Havia** muita chuva em Lisboa.

Diminutive of words

In Portuguese the diminutive of a word can also carry a touch of affection.
Adjectives like pretty – **bonito(a)**, good – **bom/boa**, etc., are often used in the
diminutive: bonit**inho(a)**, bonz**inho**/boaz**inha**. The diminutive form is usually
achieved by adding the suffix **-inho/-inha, -zinho/-zinha** to the word:

car	**carr**o – carr**inho**	little car
house	**cas**a – cas**inha**	little house
brother	**irmã**o – irmãoz**inho**	little brother
shell	**conch**a – conch**inha**	little shell

Exceptions:
c changes to **qu** as in **bar**co – **barqu**inho (little boat)
g changes to **gu** as in **jog**o – **jogu**inho (small game)

things to do

6.1 You are being asked about your daily routine. You will need these verbs
(in this order): **levantar-se, banhar-se, vestir-se, tomar, sair, ir.** Complete
the phrases below, using the present tense.

1   . . . às . . . (7.30 a.m) . . . e . . ..
2   . . . meu pequeno almoço às . . . (8 o'clock)
3   . . . de casa às . . . (8.20 am)
4   . . . ao trabalho . . . (by train)

6.2 Here is a map of Portugal. Can you say what the weather is like . . .

1   Em Lisboa
2   No Porto
3   No Algarve
4   Em Coimbra
5   No Atlântico?

Atlântico

1   nublado com aguaceiro

2   ventoso e nublado

3   um dia lindo

4   chuvoso e frio

5   ensolarado e quente

ENTERTAINMENT

Portugal offers a variety of entertainment, from cinemas, theatres, discos (**a discoteca**), opera and musicals, to the traditional bullfight (**a tourada**), folk dancing (**as danças folclóricas**) and the casinos. The elegant Cassino do Estoril is one of the most famous in the world. All casinos have a restaurant and a nightly show. Evening wear is required and foreigners must show their passport.

o cinema/the cinema

Frank is taking the children to the cinema in Lisbon that afternoon. They look in the newspaper to see what the choices are.

José: Pai, **está a passar um filme** de Walt Disney no cinema da Praça dos Restauradores. É para todos.
Frank: A escolha é tua. **Queres** assistir a este, Célia?
Célia: Sim, papai, quero. Gosto dos filmes de Walt Disney.
José: Eu também. **Vamos ver este**, então. Está decidido.
Frank: À que horas começa?
José: No jornal está marcado 'matinée às quinze horas'. Acaba às cinco.
Frank: Ah! Este é um bom horário. Se se apressarem chegaremos à tempo.
Célia: Já **estamos prontos**, pai!

61

Cinema e teatro (Cinema and theatre)

o cinema/o filme	the cinema/the film
está a passar um filme	a film is being shown
para todos	U-rated film
a escolha é tua	the choice is yours
quer/queres/querem assistir . . .?	do you want to watch . . .?
este filme	this film
Vamos ver este	Let's see this one
No jornal está marcado/diz . . .	It says in the newspaper . . .
matinée às quinze horas	matinée at 3 pm
o horário	the time/the timetable
apressar-se	to hurry
chegaremos à tempo	we'll arrive in time
estamos prontos	we are ready

Entradas (Tickets)

a entrada/o bilhete	entrance fee/ticket
entrada proibida	no admittance
a bilheteira	the ticket office
meia-entrada	half price (lit. half fee)
Quero/queremos ir . . .	I/we want to go . . .
ao cinema/ao teatro	to the cinema/theatre
Que peça/filme recomenda?	Which play/film do you recommend?
uma comédia	a comedy/farce
uma peça musical	a musical play
uma revista	a revue
Em que cinema/teatro?	In which cinema/theatre?
Há ainda bilhetes/ lugares para . . .?	Are there tickets/seats left for . . .?
hoje à noite?	tonight?
esta sessão?	this performance?
Qual é o preço das entradas?	What is the price of the tickets?

Ópera, Concerts, Ballet

Gosto/não gosto de . . .	I like/I don't like . . .
ópera/concêrto	opera/concerts
balé clássico (moderno)	classical (modern) ballet
Onde fica a sala de concêrtos?	Where is the concert hall?
a teatro/a ópera	the theatre/the opera house
Tem um programa?	Do you have a programme?
É preciso traje a rigor?	Is evening wear required?
LOTAÇÃO ESGOTADA	TICKETS SOLD OUT

Other entertainments

a discoteca/a boite/o show	disco/nightclub/show
as danças folclóricas	folk dancing
as casas de fados (o fado)	'fado' houses
a tourada/os esportes	bullfight/sports
o jogo de futebol	football match
as corridas de cavalos/automóveis	horse/motor races

EATING OUT

Traditional and typical Portuguese food is delicious, and even the unfamiliar dishes are worth trying. In general you will find the best cuisine, at good prices, in a restaurant (**um restaurante**). Restaurants are classified by a plaque fixed outside, featuring a plate (**um prato**) and up to four sets of cutlery (**talheres**), representing the four categories: **luxo** (luxury), **1a. primeira** (1st class); **2a. segunda** (2nd class); **3a. terceira** (3rd class – usually the **tascas**, a sort of bar-restaurant where the food is good and plentiful). The menu (**a ementa**) or (**a lista**) is also displayed outside.

O restaurante/the restaurant

Sra. Gomes looks after her grandchildren while Maria and Frank have an evening out in Lisbon. They go to a **Casa de Fados** where they dine to the sound of the famous **fado** songs accompanied by guitars.

Frank:	**Tem uma mesa** para dois?
Empregado:	Sim, senhor. **Venham comigo** . . . Temos esta **perto da** janela e aquela mais perto do corredor. Esta aqui é melhor.
Maria:	Pois. Ficamos com esta então. Obrigada.
Empregado:	Aqui está **a ementa e a lista dos vinhos**. Fiquem à vontade.
	(returning later to take the order)
	Já escolheram? Senhora . . .

Maria:	Sim. Traga-nos uns petiscos variados **para começar**, por favor.
Empregado:	Sim, senhora.
Maria:	**E depois** . . . humm . . . queria comer peixe. **O que recomenda?**
Empregado:	Caldeirada é a especialidade da casa. E hoje está excelente.
Maria:	Pois. Caldeirada, então.
Frank:	Eu vou comer Ensopado de Cabrito à moda da casa.
Empregado:	**E para beber?**
Frank:	Uma garrafa de vinho da casa **para mim**. E **para ti**, Maria?
Maria:	Vinho verde para mim, por favor. Meia garrafa. (45 minutes later . . .)
Empregado:	Que desejam para sobremesa?
Maria:	Uma torta de amêndoas e um pudim flan.
Empregado:	**Querem café, aperitivos?**
Maria:	Sim. Uma bica e um cálice de Moscatel, por favor.
Frank:	Vinho do Porto para mim. E **a conta**, se faz favor.

Do you have a table?

Tem uma mesa?	Do you have a table?
Para quantas pessoas?	For how many people?
para dois	for two
(Somos) quatro/oito	(We are) four/eight
Venham comigo	Come with me
Tenho/temos esta/aquela	I/we have this one/that one
perto da janela/do corredor	by the window/the corridor
Fico/ficamos com esta	I/we will take this one

Asking and ordering

Empregado! (or **Faz favor!**)	Waiter!/Waitress!
Traga-nos . . .	Bring us . . .
uns petiscos variados	a selection of appetisers
uma entrada/uma sobremesa	a starter/a dessert
a ementa/a lista dos vinhos	the menu/the wine list
Um momento, por favor, ainda não escolhi	Just a moment please, I still haven't chosen
Queria comer . . .	I'd like to eat . . .
peixe/frutos do mar	fish/seafood
carne	meat
caça e criação (aves)	game and poultry
O que me recomenda?	What do you recommend?
De que é feito/Como é este prato?	What is this dish made of?

Não gosto deste prato.	I don't like it.
Não pode trocar?	May I change it?
Podia trazer . . .?	Could you bring . . ./May I have . . .?
sal/açúcar/pimenta	salt/sugar/pepper
um guardanapo/pão	a napkin/some bread
E para beber?	And to drink?
para mim/ti	for me/you

Some dishes

sopa/salada	soup/salad
caldeirada	seafood casserole
ensopado de cabrito	kid stew
carne assada	roast beef
bacalhau	cod (traditional Portuguese speciality)

Desserts

uma sobremesa	a dessert
uma torta de amêndoas/ laranja/chocolate	an almond/orange/ chocolate tart
um pudim flan	a cream caramel
Querem café/aperitivos?	Would you like coffee/an aperitif?
Sim, uma bica	Yes, a small black coffee
um cálice de Moscatel	a small glass of Moscatel (a sweet, fortified dessert wine from Setúbal)
vinho do Porto	Port wine
vinho da Madeira	Madeira wine
um licôr	a liqueur

The bill

a conta, por favor	the bill, please
Queremos pagar separadamente	We'd like to pay separately
Acho que há um engano	I think there is a mistake
Não compreendo esta conta	I don't understand this bill
Pode explicar-me esta conta?	Can you explain this bill to me?
O serviço está incluído?	Is service included?
Guarde o trôco/Isto é para o senhor (a senhora)	Keep the change/This is for you
Muito obrigado(a), estava muito bom/ excelente	Thank you very much, it was very good/ excellent

Useful phrases

prato do dia	dish of the day
pratos regionais	local dishes
caseiro(a)	home made
à moda da casa	chef's speciality
especialidade da casa	speciality of the house

the way it works

para (for)

To say that something is for someone, just put the word **para** before the subject pronoun (**eu**, **tu**, **você**, **êle**, **ela**, **nós**, **vocês**, **êles**, **elas**). This holds good for all except for the first two: 'for me' which becomes **para *mim*** and 'for you' which becomes **para *ti***.

para meu marido/para minha filha   for my husband/for my daughter

How to say 'to start with', 'to follow'

Eu quero (or **Para mim**) sopa **para começar e depois**, carne assada.

I'd like soup *to start with* and roast beef *to follow*.

The verb **começar** (to begin/to start), is regular and is conjugated in the same way as all the regular verbs of the **-ar** group. The word **depois** means 'after' and 'later'. When it means 'later' it is used on its own, but when it's used to say 'after' it takes a preposition (**da**, **de**, **do**, **das**, **dos**):

Queria uma salada, uma caldeirada, **e depois**, um café.
    I'd like a salad, a caldeirada, *and later*, a coffee.
Eles chegaram **depois *das*** dez (horas) (fem/plural)
    They arrived *after* ten o'clock.
Depois *do* teatro (masc. sing), vamos jantar.
    After the theatre, we are going to have dinner.

things to do

6.3 You are going to the cinema. Answer the questions **a bilheteira** asks you, and put your questions to her.

Ela: Quer bilhetes para esta sessão?
You: (Yes, you do. Ask for 4: 2 adults, 2 children)
Ela: São 1400$00, por favor.
You: (Write this amount down in full)

6.4 Have a look at this menu and write in English the names of the dishes:

Ementa

- Frutos do mar variados
- Sopa de feijão verde
- Salada de batatas com ovos
- Omelete de atun
- Pato à moda da casa
- Bacalhau à Portuguesa
- Carne assada
- Torta de laranja
- Pudin flan

BUYING SOUVENIRS

umas lembranças/gifts

After the morning service at the church in Sintra, Maria remembers that she hasn't bought any gifts to take to her friends back home, and the family goes together to the souvenir shops around Sintra's main square. Célia also wants to buy something.

Maria:	Bom dia. Podemos **dar uma vista de olhos na loja?**
Vendedora:	**Sim, claro**! Fiquem à vontade.
Maria:	Queríamos umas lembrancinhas para os amigos. **Nada muito caro**, coisas simples mas típicas de Portugal.
Vendedora:	Pois! Temos galos, loiças de barro, azulejos, lenços, os bordados, as rendas, artigos de couro. . . Podem escolher à vontade. **Quando decidirem e só chamar-me.**
Maria:	Obrigada.

In the souvenir shop

Posso/podemos escolher?	Can I/can we choose?
dar uma vista de olhos na loja	look around the shop
Sim, claro!/Pois!	Yes, of course!
Claro que sim/claro que não	Of course/of course not

Fiquem à vontade	Take your time
umas lembranças/lembrancinhas	some gifts/little gifts
uns presentes	some presents
para os amigos/a família	for friends/family
nada muito caro	nothing too expensive
coisas simples	simple things
coisas típicas	typical things
coisas leves/fáceis de levar	things that are light/easy to carry
Podem escolher	choose/look around
Quando (eu) decidir/decidirem	When I/you have decided
é só chamar-me	just call me

Typical Portuguese souvenirs

os galos (o galo de Barcelos)	the Barcelos cock (symbol of an old Portuguese legend)
as loiças de barro/de porcelana	pottery/china
os azulejos	Portuguese tiles
os bordados/as rendas	embroidery/lace
os lenços/os xailes	handkerchieves/shawls
artigos de couro (cabedal)	leather goods
as filigranas	filigree jewellery
de ouro/de prata	in gold/in silver

TALKING ABOUT THINGS

agarra que é ladrão!/stop thief!

The salesgirl is busy with Maria and Célia. Frank and José are waiting for them outside, when José sees someone shoplifting. He shouts: **AGARRA QUE É LADRÃO!** Everyone hurries outside as the thief disappears up a side street. The police arrive.

Policial:	O ladrão era homem ou mulher?
José:	**Era uma mulher jovem.**
Policial:	O menino pode descrevê-la?
José:	Sim. **Ela tinha cabelos longos** e claros, **era alta** e **usava** calças compridas . . . acho que eram azul claro . . não me lembro bem . . . e blusa branca de mangas curtas.
Policial:	O menino lembra-se de mais algum detalhe?
José:	Uhnn. . . ela **usava** óculos de sol.
Policial:	Poderia descrever o que viu?

José: Ela entrou naquela loja, olhou à su volta, tirou algo daquela prateleira e **rápidamente** meteu na sua mala de mão. Quando eu gritei 'agarra que é ladrão' ela correu.

Policial: E para onde foi?

José: Foi naquela direção e logo desapareceu numa daquelas ruas.

Policial: **Obrigado pela sua ajuda. Donde é?**

José: Sou da Inglaterra.

Policial: O menino fala muito bem Português!

José: Obrigado. Minha mãe é Portuguesa, meu pai é inglês.

Policial: Ah! Sim. Adeus. **Fico-lhe muito grato.**

Describing people and things

o ladrão/a ladra	the thief
homem/mulher	man/woman
Pode descrevê-la(lo)?	Can you describe her(him)?
Poderia descrever o que viu/ o que aconteceu?	Could you describe what you saw/what happened?
Ela tinha . . .	She had . . .
cabelos longos e claros	long fair hair
era/não era alta	was/wasn't tall
usava . . .	was wearing . . .
acho que . . .	I think that . . .
acho que sim/acho que não	I think so/I don't think so
lembrar-se	to remember
não me lembro bem	I don't remember very well
não estou certo(a)	I am not sure
mais algum detalhe?	any other details?
ela usava óculos de sol	she was wearing sun glasses
Ela entrou/olhou/tirou/correu	She went in (entered)/looked/took/ran
à sua volta	around yourself
rapidamente	quickly
meter/meteu	to put/you, he, she, it put
gritar/gritei	to shout, to scream/I shouted, I screamed

OTHER PHRASES

Fala muito bem Português	You speak Portuguese very well
Obrigado (a) pela sua ajuda	Thank you for your help
Pode ajudar-me, por favor?	Can you help me, please?
Fico-lhe muito grato/grata	I am very grateful to you

Perdas e danos (Loss and theft)

PEGA LADRÃO!	STOP THIEF!
Socorro! Polícia!	Help! Police!
um/uma policial	a police officer
Fui . . .	I have been . . .
roubado(a)	robbed/mugged
atacado(a)	attacked
furtaram	he/she/they stole
Roubaram-me . . .	My . . . has been stolen
a mala de mão	handbag
a carteira	purse/wallet
Perdi-me	I am lost
Perdi . . .	I have lost . . .
os meus documentos	my documents
o meu passaporte	my passport
Onde fica o posto de polícia?	Where is the police station?
o consulado/a embaixada	the consulate/the embassy

Other emergencies

Emergência! Urgência!	Emergency!
Houve um acidente	There has been an accident
Chame uma ambulância	Call an ambulance
Chame um médico	Call a doctor
Há feridos/mortos	There are people hurt/dead
FOGO!	FIRE!
PERIGO!	DANGER!
PARE!	STOP!

the way it works

How to say you are doing something (the present continuous)

If you want to say that you *are doing* something, you use the present participle of the verb. This is formed by adding **-ando** (for **-ar** verbs), **-endo** (for **-er** verbs), or **-indo** (for **-ir** verbs) to the stem:

us**ar**	us**ando**	(wearing)
corr**er**	corr**endo**	(running)
sa**ir**	sa**indo**	(leaving)

Note: In Portugal the infinitive is more often used:

correr **a** correr	fazer **a** fazer
Ela estava a correr	Estamos a fazer compras
She was running	We are shopping

The present continuous is formed by the verb **estar** plus present participle:

Eu **estou saindo** agora	I am leaving now
Eles **estavam correndo**	They were running
Ela **esta usando** óculos	She is wearing glasses

Describing people and things

The verbs for describing things – usually **ser** and **estar** – are used in the imperfect tense when talking about the past:

Ser is followed by an adjective, e.g:
Ela era alta   She was tall.

Estar is often followed by the present participle, e.g:
Ele estava correndo, comprando, saindo, etc.

Note: The present and imperfect of the verb **ter** (to have) is also used to describe people and things, e.g:
Ela **tinha** olhos azuis   She had blue eyes
A casa **tem** jardins lindos   The house has beautiful gardens

Adverbs

Look how the endings of these adjectives change, to transform them into adverbs:

Adjective		*Adverb*	
rápido(a)	quick	rapida**mente**	quickly
gracioso(a)	graceful	graciosa**mente**	gracefully
triste	sad	triste**mente**	sadly
alegre	joyful	alegre**mente**	joyfully

Just add **-mente** to all adjectives other than those ending in the masculine(**-o**). These must be put in the feminine before adding **-mente**, as in the first two examples above

71

Stating your nationality

Look at the question the police officer asked José:
Donde é?   Where are you from?
And José's answer:
Sou da Inglaterra   I am from England

a Escócia	Scotland
a Irlanda	Ireland
o País de Gales	Wales
os Estados Unidos da America (EUA)	United States of America

Sou da Grã-Bretanha	Sou Britânico/Britânica
da Inglaterra	Inglês/Inglesa
da Escócia	Escocês/Escocesa
do País de Gales	Galês/Galesa
de Portugal	Português/Portuguesa
da Irlanda	Irlandês/Irlandesa
dos EUA	Americano/Americana
do Brasil	Brasileiro/Brasileira

Some opposites

alto(a) –	baixo(a)	tall, high –	short, low
longo(a) –	curto(a)	long –	short
gordo(a) –	magro(a)	fat –	slim
grosso(a) –	fino(a)	thick, rude –	thin, refined
grande –	pequeno(a)	big, great –	small
feio(a) –	bonito(a)	ugly –	pretty
velho(a) –	jovem	old –	young (people)
novo(a)–	velho(a)	new (things), young –	old
dentro –	fora	in(side) –	out(side)

things to do

7.1   Translate the following text into Portuguese:

In a souvenir shop

Good morning/afternoon. I'd like to see some shawls, please. In wool, cotton or silk. They (the colours) can be either black or white. And also (**também**) some embroidered handkerchiefs, and small pottery objects (**objetos**).

7.2 Translate the following text into English:

An emergency
(You are in a department store and have been robbed)

Por favor, gostaria de falar com o gerente (the manager). (He comes) Meu nome é. . . . Sou inglês. Fui roubado nesta loja há poucos (few) minutos. Roubaram-me a carteira, meu passaporte e todos os meus documentos. Pode ajudar-me? Pode chamar a polícia e o meu consulado? Este é o número do telefone. Muito obrigada/obrigado.

THANKS AND PACKING

não esqueça/don't forget . . . .

It's time to leave and the family is busy packing.

Célia:	Mãe, deixe-me **fazer a** minha **mala.**
Maria:	Está bem. **Não esqueça** os presentes. Ainda estão no saco de plástico.
José:	Célia, por acaso não vistes o novo dicionário de Português que comprei? **Não o encontro!**
Célia:	Está naquela gaveta lá.
Maria:	Frank . . . a nossa **documentação**, os **bilhetes aéreos**, os **documentos** do carro. . .
Frank:	Deixe que eu cuido disso.
José:	Pai, quem vai encarregar-se da máquina fotográfica?
Frank:	Eu mesmo, filho. Vamos deixa-la fora da mala.
Maria:	**Pronto!** As malas estão prontas e fechadas. Ufa, quanta bagagem!
Sra. Gomes:	(comes in holding some items of clothing) Maria, e estas camisolas? Não vão levá-las?
Maria:	Oh! Esqueci-me delas. **Vou ter que** abrir a mala novamente!

Packing

fazer as malas	to pack
deixe-me fazer as minhas malas	let me pack my suitcase
Não esqueça . . .	don't forget . . .
Esqueci-me delas (deles)!	I've (had) forgotten them!
ainda estão	they are still
no saco de plástico	in the plastic bag

por acaso/ao acaso/em caso de	by chance/at random/in case of
não o(a) encontro	I can't find it
naquela gaveta lá	in that drawer over there
Deixe que eu cuido disso	I will look after that
encarregar-se de	to be in charge of
eu mesmo	myself
vamos deixá-la(lo)	let's leave it
pronto!	ready! finished!
as malas estão prontas	the suitcases are ready
nós estamos prontos	we are ready
Ufa, quanta bagagem!	So much luggage!
Não vão levá-las(los)?	Aren't you taking them?
Vou ter que . . .	I'll have to . . .
abrir a mala novamente	open the suitcase again

What they are packing

os presentes	the presents
o novo dicionário de Português	the new Portuguese dictionary
a máquina fotográfica	the camera
a documentação/os documentos/os bilhetes aéreos	the documentation/the documents/the air tickets
as camisolas	the sweatshirts

adeus/goodbye

They say goodbye to their family and friends.

Frank:	Obrigado pela hospitalidade. Passamos umas férias maravilhosas.
Sra. Gomes:	O prazer foi nosso, Frank. Vamos sentir **saudades** de vocês.
Maria:	Virão visitar-nos na Inglaterra, não é?
Sra. Gomes:	Quem sabe . . . talvez em Agôsto.
José:	Venha sim, vovó. Venha conhecer a nova cidade onde moramos.
Frank:	Esperamos recebê-los em nossa nova casa.
Maria:	Adeus a todos e até breve.
All:	Adeus. Até breve. Boa viagem!

Thanks and goodbyes

Obrigado(a) pela . . .	Thank you for . . .
hospitalidade	your hospitality
acolhida/pelo acolhimento	your reception/welcoming
Passamos . . . maravilhosos(as)	We had a wonderful . . .
umas férias	. . . holiday
momentos	. . . time/moments
uma noite/um dia	. . . an evening/a day

O prazer é/foi nosso/meu	It is/was our/my pleasure
sentir saudades	to miss somebody/something
ter saudades de casa	to be homesick
Virão visitar-nos, não é?	You will visit us, won't you?
Quem sabe . . . talvez	Who knows . . . maybe/perhaps
Venha/venham sim!	Please do come!
a nova cidade/casa onde moramos	the new city/house where we live
Esperamos recebê-los (las)	We look forward to having you
Espero vê-la (lo, los, las) novamente	I look forward to seeing you again
Adeus/até breve/boa viagem	Goodbye/see you soon/have a good journey

things to do

7.3 You are leaving and you want to thank the Portuguese friends with whom you have been staying.
1. Thank them for their hospitality.
2. Say you had a lovely holiday and you hope they will come to visit you in your country.
3. Say you look forward to seeing them again.

1.1 Sim, somos./Sim, são./Sim, é./Aqui está./De nada.
1.2 1 sou. 2 somos. 3 é. 4 são. 5 sou. 6 estamos. 7 é. 8 é.
1.3 1 meu. 2 seu. 3 nossa. 4 nossos. 5 minha. 6 suas.
1.4 (a) 2. (b) 5. (c) 3. (d) 1. (e) 4.

2.1 1 Tenho vinte anos. 2 Sim, tenho . . .; Não, não tenho. 3 Tem . . .
2.2 1a. Estação de Santa Apolónia. 2a. Sé. 3a. Estação do Rossio.
2.3 1 À que horas é o pequeno almoço? Das oito às dez. 2 À que horas chega o seu amigo (a sua amiga)? Chega às sete e um quarto (or sete e quinze). 3 À que horas parte o comboio? Parte às quinze e trinta. 4 À que horas abre o museu? Abre às nove e quarenta e cinco./Abre às quinze para as dez/às dez menos um quarto/às dez menos quinze./Abre um quarto para as dez.

3.1 Dois bilhetes para Coimbra, segunda classe./Hoje. Quero dois bilhetes de ida e volta./Quanto custa o bilhete de segunda classe no expresso?/ Não fumadores. À que horas parte o comboio?/Parte do cais número dois dentro de vinte minutos?
3.2 4, 1. 2. 6. 5. 3. 8. 7.
3.3 1 cinquenta e cinco escudos e vinte e cinco centavos 2 trezentos e trinta escudos 3 dois mil e quinhentos escudos
4 mil duzentos e cinquenta escudos   5 quinhentos e quarenta e cinco escudos.
3.4 1 Maria vai para o hotel 2 Célia e José vão ao correio 3 Nós vamos ao banco.
4 Eu vou para o aeroporto.

4.1 1 comprar sapatos. 2 um pacote de biscoitos. 3 comprar uma gravata e umas calças compridas. 4 quer comprar Melhoral. 5 quer comprar peixe, carne e um quilo de tomates.
4.2 1 à sapataria. 2 biscoitos no supermercado. 3 a boutique (or loja de roupas).
4 na farmácia. 5 à peixaria, ao talho, e à quitanda.
4.3 1 meia dúzia de ovos. 2 cem gramas de queijo. 3 uma garrafa de vinho tinto.
4 duzentos gramas de presunto. 5 meio quilo de tomates. 6 um pacote de manteiga.
4.4 1 Sim, gostam. 2 Não, não gosto. 3 Sim, ela gosta muito. 4 Sim, gostamos.
4.5 1 Telefonista, quero fazer uma chamada (quero ligar) para a Inglaterra.
2 número oito-zero-um-cinco-dois-seis. 3 Ligação/chamada à cobrar no destino, por favor.
4.6 1 Sim, já/Não, ainda não. 2 Sim, êles/elas ainda estão aqui. 3 Sim, êles/elas já fizeram as malas. 4 Não, nós ainda não fizemos as malas.

5.1 Bom dia/boa tarde. Tenho uma dôr no estômago(dói-me o estômago). Pode recomendar-me algo?/Esta manhã. Acho que comi algo que me fêz mal (que não me fez bem)./ O que recomenda?/ Quantos devo tomar e quantas vêzes por ao dia?
5.2 1 When did you start to feel unwell? 2 He thought I had a stomach upset.
3 Some tablets. Take one three times a day.
5.3 1 Tenho uma dôr de cabeça (dói-me a cabeça). 2 Tenho uma dôr neste dente (dói-me este dente). 3 Pode(poderia) recomendar-me um médico? 4 Eu vomitei.
5 Não me sinto bem (sinto-me mal). 6 Onde há uma farmácia? 7 Estou doente.
5.4 1 de cabeça. 2 de dente. 3 nas costas. 4 no estômago.
5.5 headaches, fever, cold and flu
5.6 1 Meu carro está avariado. Pode verificar? 2 Tenho um pneu vazio(Um pneu está vazio). 3 Pode verificar o óleo e a àgua, por favor? 4 O motor aquece (está a aquecer) demais.
5.7 1 Danger! Stop! 2 Caution! Pedestrian Crossing! 3 Toll in 500 metres. 4 No Traffic (Traffic not allowed).

KEY TO EXERCISES

6.1   1 Levanto-me às sete e meia (sete e trinta), banho-me e visto-me. 2 Tomo . . .
às oito horas. 3 Saio . . . às oito e vinte. 4 Vou . . . de comboio.
6.2   1 cloudy with showers 2 windy and cloudy 3 a lovely day 4 rainy and cold
5 sunny and hot
6.3   Sim, por favor. Quero quatro: dois adultos e duas crianças./mil e quatrocentos
escudos.
6.4   a selection of seafood/green bean soup/potato and egg salad/tuna omelette/
chef's duck speciality/cod Portuguese style/roast beef/orange tart/cream caramel.

7.1   Bom dia/boa tarde. Queria ver alguns xailes, se faz favor. Em lã, algodão ou
seda. As côres podem ser preto ou branco. Também alguns lenços bordados e
pequenos objetos de barro.
7.2   I'd like to speak to the manager, please. My name is. . . . . I am English. My
wallet, passport, and all my documents have been stolen in this shop a few minutes
ago. Can you help me? Can(could) you call the police and the British consulate?
This(here) is the telephone number. Thank you very much.
7.3   1 Muito obrigado(-a) pela sua hospitalidade(acolhida). 2 Passei umas férias
maravilhosas. Espero que venha(venham) visitar-me(-nos) na(no). . . 3 Espero vê-
lo(-la, -los, -las) novamente.

VOCABULARY

Numbers 0–100

0 zero	11 onze	22 vinte e dois/duas	40 quarenta
1 um/uma	12 doze	23 vinte e três	50 cinquenta
2 dois/duas	13 treze	24 vinte e quatro	60 sessenta
3 três	14 catorze	25 vinte e cinco	70 setenta
4 quatro	15 quinze	26 vinte e seis	80 oitenta
5 cinco	16 dezasseis	27 vinte e sete	90 noventa
6 seis	17 dezassete	28 vinte e oito	100 cem/cento
7 sete	18 dezoito	29 vinte e nove	cem becomes cento in
8 oito	19 dezanove	30 trinta	front of another number.
9 nove	20 vinte	31 trinta e um	
10 dez	21 vinte e um	32 trinta e dois/duas	

Numbers 101–1000

101 cento e um/uma	300 trezentos	700 setecentos
150 cento e cinquenta	400 quatrocentos	800 oitocentos
200 duzentos	500 quinhentos	900 novecentos
250 duzentos e cinquenta	600 seiscentos	1000 mil/um conto

Ordinals

first	primeiro/a	fifth	quinto/a	ninth	nono/a
second	segundo/a	sixth	sexto/a	tenth	décimo/a
third	terceiro/a	seventh	sétimo/a		
fourth	quarto/a	eighth	oitavo/a		

Higher numbers

1.550	mil quinhentos e cinquenta	31.460 trinta e um mil,
2.000	dois mil	quatrocentos e sessenta
10.000	dez mil/dez contos	

Months of the year (os meses do ano)

January	Janeiro	July	Julho
February	Fevereiro	August	Agosto
March	Março	September	Setembro
April	Abril	October	Outubro
May	Maio	November	Novembro
June	Junho	December	Dezembro

The seasons (as estações do ano)

Spring	a Primavera
Summer	o Verão
Autumn	o Outono
Winter	o Inverno

VOCABULARY

The time (o tempo)

day	o dia
month	o mês
year	o ano
week	a semana
weekend	o fim de semana
clock	o relógio
hour	a hora
minute	o minuto
second	o segundo

Colours (as côres)

black	preto/a	pink	côr-de-rosa
blue	azul	purple	roxo/a
brown	castanho	red	vermelho/a
green	verde	silver	prateado/a
grey	cinzento/a	white	branco/a
golden	dourado/a	yellow	amarelo/a
navy blue	azul marinho	light	claro/a
mauve	lilás	dark	escuro/a

Clothes and accessories (roupas e ascessórios)

bag	a saca	dress	o vestido
belt	o cinto	gloves	as luvas
blouse	a blusa	handbag	a mala de mão
bra	o soutien	hat	o chapéu
briefs/pants	as calças	jacket	a jaqueta
coat	o casaco	jeans	os jeans
jumper	a camisola de malha	suit	o fato
nightdress	a camisola de dormir	swimming costume	o fato de banho
pyjamas	o pijama	tie	a gravata
raincoat	a capa de chuva	tights	o collant
scarf	o lenço de pescoço	tracksuit	o fato de corrido
		trousers	as calças compridas
shirt	a camisa	t-shirt	a camiseta
shorts	os calções	underpants	as cuecas
skirt	a saia	umbrella	o guarda-chuva
slip	a saia de baixo	vest (Brit.)	a camisola interior
socks	as peúgas	waistcoat	o colete
stockings	as meias		

Shoes

boots	as botas	shoes	os sapatos
sandals	as sandálias	trainers	os ténis

Shops (as lojas)

antique shop	o antiquário	dry cleaner's	a tinturaria
bank	o banco	hairdresser's	o cabelereiro
bookshop	a livraria	jeweller's	a ourivesaria
chemist's	a farmacia	shoemaker's	o sapateiro
clothes shop	a boutique	stationer's	a papelaria
		toyshop	a loja de brinquedos

VOCABULARY

Jeweller's (ourivesaria)

bangle	o bracelete	earrings	os brincos
bracelet	a pulseira	filigree jewellery	as filigranas
brooch	o broche	necklace	o colar
chain	a corrente	pendant	o pingente
clock/watch	o relógio	ring	o anel
cross	a cruz		

At the chemist's

antiseptic	o anti-séptico	indigestion	o remédio para
contraceptive	o contraceptivo	remedy	indigestão
dressing	o curativo	painkiller	o analgésico
cotton wool	o algodão	plasters	os pensos rapidos
desinfectant	o desinfectante	tablet	o comprimido
gauze	a gaze	throat pastilles	as pastilhas para a garganta

Toiletries and cosmetics

blusher	o blush	cleansing.	creme de limpeza
comb/hair brush	o pente/a escova de cabelos	moisturising	creme hidratante
cream	o creme	hand cream	creme para as mãos
deodorant	o desodori-zante	shampoo	o shampoo
diapers, nappies	as fraldas	shaving cream	o creme de barbear
emery board	a lima de unhas	soap	o sabonete
lipstick	o batôn	suntan cream	o bronzeador
razor blade	a lâmina de barbear	tissues	os lenços de papel
sanitary towels	os pensos higiênicos	toilet paper	o papel higiênico
		toothbrush	a escova de dentes
		toothpaste	a pasta de dentes

Food shops

baker's	a padaria	greengrocer's	a quitanda
butcher's	o talho	grocery	a mercearia
cake shop	a pastelaria	market	o mercado
delicatessen	a salsicharia	supermarket	o supermercado
fishmonger's	a peixaria		

Fish (peixe)

clams	as amêijoas	mussels	os mexilhões
cod	o bacalhau	mackerel	a cavala
crab	o caranguejo	oysters	as ostras
king prawns	as gambas	octopus	o polvo
lobster	a lagosta		

sardines	as sardinhas	squid	as lulas
shrimp	os camarões	trout	a truta
sea bass	o robalo	tuna	o atum
sole	o linguado	whiting	a pescada

Vegetables (os legumes)

aubergine	a berinjela	lentils	as lentilhas
beans	o feijão	lettuce	a alface
runner beans	o feijão verde/as vagens	mushrooms	os cogumelos
		onions	as cebolas
carrot	a cenoura	potatoes	as batatas
cauliflower	a couve-flor	pumpkin	a abóbora
chick peas	o grão de bico	peas	as ervilhas
cucumber	o pepino	radishes	os rabanetes
garlic	o alho	spinach	os espinafres
kale/cabbage	a couve portuguesa	tomatoes	os tomates
		turnips	os nabos
leek	o alho porro	(white) cabbage	o repolho

Fruit (as frutas)

almonds	as amêndoas	lime	a lima
apple	a maçã	melon	o melão
banana	a banana	orange	a laranja
coconut	o côco	peach	o pêssego
cherry	a cereja	pear	a pera
figs	os figos	pineapple	o ananás
grapes	as uvas	plums	as ameixas
lemon	o limão	prunes	as ameixas secas
		raspberries	as framboesas
		strawberries	os morangos
		walnuts	as nozes

Meat, game, poultry (carne, caça e criação)

bacon	o toucinho	partridge	a perdiz
beef	a carne	pheasant	o faisão
chicken	o frango	sucking pig	o leitão
duck	o pato	pigeon	o pombo
goose	o ganso	quail	a codorniz
hare	a lebre	rabbit	o coelho
kid	o cabrito	steak	o bife
kidneys	os rins	sausage	a salsicha
liver	o fígado	tongue	a lingua
mutton	o carneiro	turkey	o peru
		venison	o veado

VOCABULARY

Tobacconist's (a tabacaria)

candy	os rebuçados	cigarettes	os cigarros
chewing gum	as pastilhas elásticas	cigars	os charutos
		lighter	o isqueiro
chewing tobacco	o tabaco de mascar	matches	os fósforos
		pipe	o cachimbo

Professions (as profissões)

accountant	contador(a)	housewife	dona de casa
architect	arquiteto(a)	journalist	jornalista
bank clerk	bancário(a)	lawyer	advogado(a)
businessman	homem de negócios	librarian	bibliotecário(a)
		manager	gerente/diretor(a)
civil servant	funcionário(a) público(a)	nurse	enfermeiro(a)
		painter	pintor(a)
director	diretor(a)	sales rep.	representante
doctor	doutor(a) médico(a)	shop assistant	vendedor(a)
		student	estudante
driver	motorista	secretary	secretária
employee	empregado(a)	teacher	professor(a)
engineer	engenheiro(a)	technician	técnico(a)

Workplaces

I work in a/an . . .	Eu trabalho num/ numa . . .	factory	(a) fábrica
		hospital	(o) hospital
bank	(o) banco	college	(o) colégio
library	(a) biblioteca	office	(o) escritório
market	(o) mercado	school	(a) escola
		shop	(a) loja

Table setting

bowl	a tijela	plate	o prato
cup	a xícara	spoon	a colher
fork	o garfo	tablecloth	a toalha de mesa
glass	o copo	teaspoon	a colherinha
knife	a faca		

Parts of the body

ankle	o tornozelo	hand	a mão
arm	o braço	head	a cabeça
back	as costas	heart	o coração
blood	o sangue	kidney	o rin
bone	o osso	knee	o joelho
breast	o seio	leg	a perna
ear	a orelha/o ouvido	mouth	a boca
eye	o olho	nose	o nariz
face	o rosto	rib	a costela
finger	o dedo	shoulder	o ombro
foot	o pé	skin	a pele
hair	o cabelo	stomach	o estômago

Parts of the car

battery	a bateria	lights	as luzes
brakes	os travões	radiator	o radiador
carburettor	o carburador	steering wheel	o volante
clutch	a embraiagem	tyres	os pneus
engine	o motor	wheels	as rodas
exhaust	o cano de escape	windscreen	o párabrisa
headlight	o farol		
ignition	a ignição		

Places and Architecture

botanical gardens	o Jardim Botânico	harbour	o porto
bridge	a ponte	monastery	o mosteiro
castle	o castelo	monument	o monumento
city centre	o centro da cidade	museum	o museu
chapel	a capela	old town	a cidade velha
church	a igreja	palace	o palácio
convent	o convento	park	o parque
flea market	a feira da ladra	ruins	as ruínas
fortress	a fortaleza		

Landscapes

cave	a caverna	mountain	a montanha
hill	a colina	river	o rio
island	a ilha	sea	o mar
lake	o lago	valley	o vale

VOCABULARY

Portuguese – English Vocabulary

Note: (*m*) = masculine, (*f*) = feminine, (*pl*) = plural, (*adj*) = adjective

à tabela on time
à vontade (ficar a . . .) (be at) ease, informal
aberto/a open
abrir to open
acampar to camp
acho que I think that
acidente (*m*) accident
acolhida (*f*) reception, welcome
açúcar (*m*) sugar
adeus (*m*) goodbye, farewell
adulto (*m*) adult
aéreos of the air; **bilhetes** – air tickets
agora now
àgua (*f*) water
aguaceiro (*m*) shower (rain)
àgua potável (*f*) drinking water
aí there
ainda still; yet
ajuda (*f*) help, assistance
alegre happy
alegria (*f*) happiness
alérgico/a allergic
alfândega (*f*) customs
algo something
algum/alguma some, any; **alguma coisa** something
alí there
almoçar to lunch
almoço (*m*) lunch
alto/a high, tall
alugar to rent, hire
amanhã tomorrow
amável nice, kind
ambulância (*f*) ambulance
amêndoa (*f*) almond
amigo/a (*m/f*) friend
anos (*m.pl*) years
ao to the, for the
apanhar to seize, catch, collect; to be beaten
aperitivo (*m*) aperitif
apertado tight
apertar to pinch, tighten; – **a mão** to shake hands
aquecer to warm up, to heat up
aquele/aquela that one
aqui here; – **tem** here is, here it is
ar (*m*) air
artigo (*m*) article

às bolas spotted, dotted
às compras shopping; **ir às** – to go shopping
áspero rough
às riscas striped
assinar to sign
atacar to attack
até breve see you soon
atrasado/a late
autocarro (*m*) bus
avaria (*f*) damage, breakdown
avariado damaged, broken down(car)
avião (*m*) airplane
avô, avó grandfather, grandmother
azul marinho navy blue
azulejos (*m.pl*) ceramic tiles

bagagem (*f*) luggage, baggage
bairro (*m*) district
baixo low; short
banco (*m*) bank
bar (*m*) bar, snack bar
barato inexpensive, cheap
barro (*m*) clay; **Louça de** – earthenware
beleza (*f*) beauty
bem well; – **feito** well done; **está** – it's all right
bica (*f*) small black coffee
bilhetaria (*f*) ticket office
bilhete (*m*) ticket; – **aéreos** air tickets
boa noite good night; – **tarde** good evening; – **viagem** have a good journey
bola (*f*) ball
bolo (*m*) cake
bom/boa good; **bom dia** good day, good morning
branco (*m*)(*adj*) white

cabeça (*f*) head
cabedal (*m*) leather
cabelos (*m.pl*) hair
cabine telefônica (*f*) telephone box
cada each
café (*m*) coffee
cais (*m*) platform, quay
caixa (*f*) cash desk, box
cálice (*m*) small glass for aperitif
calmo calm, peaceful

calor (*m*) heat
cama (*f*) bed
cambio (*m*) exchange
caminhar to walk
caminho (*m*) the way
camioneta (*f*) coach
campo de tênis (*m*) tennis court
canto (*m*) song, corner
caravana (*f*) caravan
carne (*f*) meat, flesh
caro expensive, costly
carro (*m*) car
carta (*f*) letter, card, chart; – **de condução** (*f*) driving licence
cartão de crédito (*m*) credit card
carteira (*f*) wallet
casa (*f*) house; – **de banho** (*f*) bathroom
casal (*m*) couple, married couple
caseiro/a home-made, homely
cavalo (*m*) horse
centro (*m*) centre
certeza (*f*) assurance; **com** – certainly
certo/a correct; **estar** – to be right
chá (*m*) tea
chapa (*f*) token, plate
chapéu (*m*) hat
chamar to call; **chamada telefônica** telephone call
chave (*f*) key
chega! enough!
chegar to arrive
cheio full
cheque (*m*) cheque
chuva (*f*) rain
chuveiro (*m*) shower
cidade (*f*) city, town
cinema (*m*) cinema
claro! of course
classe (*f*) class
coisa (*f*) thing
colocar to put, place
com certeza certainly, surely
comboio (*m*) train
começar to start, begin
comer to eat
comida (*f*) meal, food
comigo with me
como? how?
comprar to buy
comprimido (*m*) pill, tablet
concha (*f*) shell
conduzir to drive; to lead
conhecer to know
consulado (*m*) consulate

consulta (**marcar uma . . .**) (*f*) (make an) appointment
consultório (*m*) surgery
conta (*f*) bill
continuar to continue, carry on
conto (**um**) one thousand escudos
copo (*m*) drinking glass
côr (*f*) colour
correio (*m*) post office
corrente (*f*) chain
correr to run
correspondência (*f*) mail
couro (*m*) leather
crédito (*m*) credit
criança (*f*) child
curto/a short

dança (*f*) dance
dançar to dance
daquele(s), daquela(s) of that, of those
decidir to decide
defeito (*m*) defect
deitar to lie down
dele(s), dela(s) his, her, their
delicioso/a delicious
demais too much
demorar to be late
dentadura (*f*) denture
dente (*m*) tooth
dentista (*m*) dentist
dentro inside
depois after, afterwards
depressa fast
descrever to describe
desculpe(-me) excuse me
detalhe (*m*) detail
devagar slow
dia (*m*) day
diabético/a diabetic
dieta (*f*) diet
dinheiro (*m*) money
direçao (*f*) direction
direita right; **à** – on the right
direto straight on, direct
documentação (*f*) documentation
documentos (*m.pl*) documents
doente (*adj*) ill
doente (*m/f*) the patient
doi-me it hurts
dólar (*m*) dollar
donde? where?
dor (*f*) pain, ache
doutor/a doctor
do/da/de of, from

VOCABULARY

dúzia (*f*) dozen

electricidade (*f*) electricity
elétrico (*m*) tram
ele/ela he/she
em in, at; **– que?** where? in which?
ementa (*f*) the menu
emergência (*f*) emergency
empurre push
encarregar-se to be in charge of
encomenda (*f*) order, parcel, package
encontrar to meet, to find
enganar to deceive, to trick
engano (*m*) mistake
ensopado (*m*) stew, casserole
então then; **desde –** since then; **até –** till then
entrada (*f*) entry, entrance, ticket
equipado/a equipped
errado wrong
escolher to choose
especialidade (*f*) speciality
esposa (*f*) wife
esquecer to forget
esquerda left; **à –** on the left
esquina (*f*) corner
esse/essa that one
estação (*f*) station **– de serviço** (*f*) service station
estacionar to park, to pull up
estampado/a printed (material), patterned
estar to be
este/esta this one
estilo (*m*) style
eu I
examinar to examine
explicar to explain
é is
e and

fácil easy
família (*f*) family
farmácia (*f*) pharmacy, chemist's shop
febre (*f*) fever
fechar to close
fechado/a closed
feio/a ugly
férias (*f.pl*) holidays
ficar to remain, to stay; **– com** to keep; **fica bem** it suits, it fits; **fica-te bem** it suits you
ficha (*f*) form; **preencher uma –** to fill in a form; token (for telephone box); plug (elect.)

filho/a son/daughter
filigrana (*f*) filigree
filme (*m*) film
fim (*m*) end
fogo fire
folheto (*m*) leaflet
fome (*f*) hunger
fora out, outside
forte strong
fraco weak
frio/a cold
fruta (*f*) fruit
fumadores (*m.pl*) smokers; smoking compartment
fumar to smoke
funcionário/a civil servant, official
furado punctured, pierced
furtar to steal

garçon (*m*) waiter
garrafa (*f*) bottle
gasolina (*f*) petrol
gaveta (*f*) drawer
gelado (*m*) ice-cream
gengiva (*f*) gum
gente (*f*) people
gerência (*f*) management
gerente (*m*) manager
gostar to like
gostaria would like
grande big, great
grato/a grateful
gritar to shout, scream
grito (*m*) shout, scream
guardanapo (*m*) napkin, serviette
guia (*m*) guide

há there is, there are
hoje today
homem (*m*) man
hora (*f*) hour
horário (*m*) timetable
horrível horrible
hospital (*m*) hospital
hospitalidade (*f*) hospitality

igual equal, the same
ingrato/a ungrateful
ir to go

já already, now; **desde –** henceforth
janela (*f*) window
jardim (*m*) garden
jogo (*m*) game

jornal (*m*) newspaper
jovem (*adj*) young; **jovem** (*m/f*) the younster

lá there
ladra (*f*) female thief
ladrão (*m*) thief, robber
lamento I am sorry
largo wide
lata (*f*) tin can
lavar to wash
lembrança (*f*) souvenir
lembrar to remember
lenço (*m*) scarf, handkerchief
lentes de contacto (*f.pl*) contact lenses
levar to take; **leve-me** take me
leve light
libra (*f*) **esterlina** pound sterling
lindo/a beautiful
lingua (*f*) language, tongue
liquidação (*f*) sale, bargain
liso(a) smooth
lista (*f*) list, menu
litro (*m*) litre (1.75 pints)
logo soon
loja (*f*) shop
longe far
longo(a) long
lugar (*m*) place

mãe/mamãe (*f*) mother/mum
mais more, else; **– ou menos** more or less; **– tarde** later, later on
mas but
mala (*f*) suitcase; **– de mão** handbag
manga (*f*) sleeve
mangueira (*f*) hose-pipe; mangotree
mão (*f*) hand
mapa (*m*) map
máquina (*f*) machine
mar (*m*) sea
maravilhoso/a marvelous, wonderful
marido (*m*) husband
medicamento (*m*) medicine, remedy
médico (*m*) doctor
medidas (*f.pl*) measurements
meio (*m*) middle; **no – da rua** in the middle of the road
meio/meia half
melhor (*m*) the best; **melhor** (*adj*) better, best
melhorar to improve, to get better
menino/a boy/girl
menos less

mesa (*f*) table
mesmo, mesma same
meu, minha mine
minutos (*m.pl*) minutes
moderno/a modern
moedas (*f.pl*) coins
morar to live
mostre-me show me
motor (*m*) engine
motorista (*m/f*) driver
muito very, very much
mulher (*f*) woman, wife
música (*f*) music

nada nothing; **de –** don't mention it
nadar to swim
não no; **– há** there isn't, there aren't; **– percebo** I don't understand
naquele/a in/on/at that
neste(s), nesta(s) in this/these, on this/these
nome (*m*) name
notas (*f.pl*) notes
novamente again
no/na in/on/at the
novo/a new, young
num,numa in/on a

objecto (*m*) object
obrigado/a thank you
óculos (*m.pl*) spectacles, glasses
olá hi, hello
olhar to look at, to observe
omelete (*m*) omelette
onde? where is?; **onde está?** where is?
ontem yesterday
os/as the
ou or
ouro (*m*) gold
outro(a) another one

pacote (*m*) parcel
pagar to pay
peixe (*m*) fish
pai/papai (*m*) father, dad
país (*m*) country
pão (*m*) bread
par (*m*) pair
para to, for; **– mim** for me/to me; **– ti** for you/to you
paragem de autocarro (*f*) bus stop
pare stop
parque (*m*) park; **– de campismo** (*m*) camp site

VOCABULARY

partir to leave
partir-se to break
passante (*m*) passer-by
passaporte (*m*) passport
pegar to hold, to take
pelo/a by, for, at, on, through
pensão (*f*) boarding house
pensar to think; **penso que** I think that
pequeno small; **– almoço** breakfast
perda (*f*) loss
perder to lose, miss
perigo (*m*) danger
perto near, close
pesado heavy
pessoa (*f*) person
petiscos (*m.pl*) appetisers
pimenta (*f*) pepper
pior (*m*) the worst; **pior** (*adj*) worse, worst
plástico (*m*) plastic; **plástica(o)** made of plastic
pneu (*m*) tyre
pois because, then, so; **– claro!** of course!
polícia (*f*) police
por by, through, for; **– acaso** by chance; **– favor** please
porcelana porcelain, bone china
porque because; **por que?** why?
postal (*adj*) postal; **postal** (*m*) postcard
pouco/a little, a little, few
pousada (*f*) inn, hotel
praça (*f*) square(in a city)
praia (*f*) beach, seaside
prata (*f*) silver
prateleira (*f*) shelf
prato (*m*) plate
prazer (*m*) pleasure
preciso I need; **é –** it's necessary
preço (*m*) price
presente (*m*) present, gift
problema (*m*) problem
programa (*m*) programme
proibido/a forbidden, not allowed
pronto/a ready, finished
provar to prove
próximo/a next; **estar – de** to be close to
puxe pull

qual/quais? which?
quando? when?
quanto é?/quanto custa? how much is it?/what does it cost?

quantos/as? how many?
quarto (*m*) room
que who, whom, which; **o quê?** what?; **Que bom!** Great! Good!; **Que pena!** What a pity!
quem? who?
Quem sabe? Who knows?
quente hot
querer to want; **quer, querem?** do you want?

radiador (*m*) radiator
rápido fast
raquete (*f*) tennis racket
receber to receive
receita (*f*) prescription; recipe
receitar to prescribe
recepção (*f*) reception
recibo (*m*) receipt
recomendar to recommend
registrar to register (a letter); to record
remédio (*m*) medicine, remedy
renda (*f*) lace
repetir repeat
repousar,to rest; **repouso** (*m*) rest
reservar to reserve; **reservado/a** reserved
residencial (*adj*) residential
restaurante (*m*) restaurant
revista (*f*) magazine
roubar to steal
rua (*f*) road, street

saída (*f*) exit, way out; **– de emergência** (*f*) emergency exit
sal (*m*) salt
sala (*f*) sitting room; **– de jantar** dining room
salada (*f*) salad
salto (*m*) **raso/alto** flat/high heels
saudade (*f*) longing for someone/ something
saudável healthy, wholesome
saúde (*f*) health
se faz favor please
sêde (*f*) thirsty
seguro de saúde (*m*) health insurance
selo (*m*) stamp; seal
sem without
semana (*f*) week
sempre always
senhor/senhora Mr/Mrs, Miss
sentir to feel
separado/a apart, separated

VOCABULARY

ser to be
serviço (*m*) service; job, work
servir to serve; to fit, be suitable
seu(s) your, yours
sim yes
simpático(a) nice, kind, pleasant
simples simple; single(ticket)
sinal (*m*) signal; sign
sobremesa (*f*) dessert
socorro (*m*) help
sol (*m*) sun
sopa (*f*) soup
sorte (*f*) luck, fortune

talher (*m*) set of knife, fork and spoon;
   talheres (*m.pl*) cutlery
talvez maybe, perhaps
também also, too
teatro (*m*) theatre
tecido (*m*) material, fabric
telefone (*m*) telephone; **a ligação/
   chamada telefônica** telephone call
telefonista (*f*) operator
tempo (*m*) time; weather
tenda (*f*) tent
tenho I have
todos/todas/tudo all, every
tomar to take
torta (*f*) tart; cake
trabalho (*m*) work, job
traje a rigor (*m*) evening wear
trânsito (*m*) traffic
trazer to bring
triste sad
tristeza (*f*) sadness
trocar to change, exchange; **troco** I
   change
troco (*m*) change(money)

um/uma one, a, an
uma ligação/chamada a phone call
um momento one(just a) moment
usar to wear; to use

vasamento (*m*) leak
vazio empty
velho/a old
vendedor/a salesman/woman
vender to sell
vento (*m*) wind
ver to see, look
verdade (*f*) the truth; **verdade?** really?
   Is that true?
verificar to verify, check
vestir to dress
vez/vezes (*f*) time/times; **uma vez** once;
   duas vezes twice
viajar to travel; **viagem** (*f*) trip, journey
vida (*f*) life
visita (*f*) guest
visitar to visit
vitrine (*f*) shop-window
viver to live
voltar to come back, return
vontade (*f*) will, desire; **à** – at ease,
   comfortable; **fique à** – make yourself
   comfortable

xadrez (*m*) chess board (*adj*)
   chequered
xaile (*m*) shawl